JOURNAL FOR THE STUDY OF THE OLD TESTAMENT SUPPLEMENT SERIES
259

Editors
David J.A. Clines
Philip R. Davies

Executive Editor
John Jarick

COPENHAGEN INTERNATIONAL SEMINAR
5

General Editors
Thomas L. Thompson
Niels Peter Lemche

Associate Editors
Frederick H. Cryer
Mogens Müller
Hakan Ulfgard

Sheffield Academic Press

The Royal God

Enthronement Festivals
in Ancient Israel and Ugarit?

Allan Rosengren Petersen

Journal for the Study of the Old Testament
Supplement Series 259

Copenhagen International Seminar 5

Published by Sheffield Academic Press Ltd
Mansion House
19 Kingfield Road
Sheffield S11 9AS
England

Printed on acid-free paper in Great Britain
by Bookcraft Ltd
Midsomer Norton, Bath

British Library Cataloguing in Publication Data

A catalogue record for this book is available
from the British Library

ISBN 1-85075-864-6

CONTENTS

PREFACE AND ACKNOWLEDGMENTS

This book is a revised edition of my prize essay which I delivered to the University of Copenhagen in January 1992. I have been able to include some, but not all, of the relevant scholarly literature which has appeared after that date. I especially regret not to have been able to include Mark S. Smith's commentary on the Baal-cycle.

I wish to express my gratitude to a distinguished quartet of Old Testament scholars (or, as some would have it, the Copenhagen Gang of Four): Professor Niels Peter Lemche, from whom I learned Ugaritic, Aramaic and Akkadian, and with whom I have spent many a pleasant hour in small colloquia; Professor Thomas L. Thompson, whose friendly and useful criticism has much improved this book; Frederick Harris Cryer (Associate Professor for Research), who has had the unpleasant task of revising the English of my manuscript—unpleasant, not so much because of my English, but because I had not been aware that quotations from non-English scholarly literature should also be rendered in English; and Professor John Strange for having nourished my interest in archaeology—without him introducing me to archaeology, I would have missed many a detail of the excavation reports.

I am also very grateful to Associate Professor Mogens Trolle Larsen from the Carsten Niebuhr Institute, who has revised the Akkadian passages in this book. His corrections and suggestions have been very valuable for me.

In all this, however, I am to blame for any mistake or inaccuracy that might remain.

Since this is, in fact, my first written work delivered to the University of Copenhagen, I am very happy and fortunate to be able to present it in this form. I wish to thank Sheffield Academic Press and the editors of Copenhagen International Seminar, Niels Peter Lemche and Thomas L. Thompson, for accepting the manuscript for publication. Also many thanks to all those at the Press who have miraculously transformed my floppy disks into one of those so very familiar green books.

The publication of this book was made possible through the generous support of the Institute of Biblical Exegesis at the University of Copenhagen. Acknowledgment is due to Librairie Orientaliste Paul Geuthner, Paris, for the reproduction of the two plates from Schaeffer's excavation reports on Ugarit.

Last, but not least, I wish to extend my thanks to *Det Lyngbeckske Soranerlegat* which so generously supported me economically during my time as a student at the Faculty of Theology in the University of Copenhagen—even during the periods in which I wasn't very productive in any measurable kind of way.

Allan Rosengren Petersen
Princeton, January 1998

ABBREVIATIONS

AHw	Wolfram von Soden, *Akkadisches Handwörterbuch* (Wiesbaden: Harrassowitz, 1959–81)
ANET	James B. Pritchard (ed.), *Ancient Near Eastern Texts Relating to the Old Testament* (Princeton: Princeton University Press, 3rd edn, 1969)
AnOr	Analecta orientalia
ANVAO	Avhandlinger utgitt av Det Norske Videnskaps-Akademi i Oslo
AOAT	Alter Orient und Altes Testament
AOT	Hugo Gressmann (ed.), *Altorientalische Texte zum Alten Testament* (Berlin and Leipzig: Walter de Gruyter, 2nd edn, 1926)
ARTU	Johannes C. de Moor, *An Anthology of Religious Texts from Ugarit* (NISABA, 16; Leiden: E.J. Brill, 1987)
ATD	Das Alte Testament Deutsch
BAH	Bibliothèque archéologique et historique
BETL	Bibliotheca ephemeridum theologicarum lovaniensium
BFCT	Beiträge zur Förderung Christlicher Theologie
BKAT	Biblischer Kommentar: Altes Testament
BSGW	Berichte über die Verhandlungen der Sächsischen Gesellschaft der Wissenschaften
BZ	*Biblische Zeitschrift*
BZAW	Beihefte zur *ZAW*
CAD	Ignace I. Gelb *et al.* (eds.), *The Assyrian Dictionary of the Oriental Institute of the University of Chicago* (Chicago: Oriental Institute, 1964–)
CTA	A. Herdner (ed.), *Corpus des tablettes en cunéiformes alphabétiques découvertes à Ras Shamra–Ugarit de 1929 à 1939* (Paris: Imprimerie nationale, Geuthner, 1963)
DBSup	*Dictionnaire de la Bible, Supplément*
DT	Daily Telegraph Collection, British Museum (text collection)
DTT	*Dansk teologisk tidsskrift*
FRLANT	Forschungen zur Religion und Literatur des Alten und Neuen Testaments
GAG	Wolfram von Soden, *Grundriß der akkadischen Grammatik* (AnOr, 33; Rome: Pontificium Institutum Biblicum, 1952)

HAL	Ludwig Koehler and Walter Baumgartner, *Hebräisches und aramäisches Lexikon zum Alten Testament* (Leiden: E.J. Brill, 1967–91)
HKAT	Handkommentar zum Alten Testament
HUCA	*Hebrew Union College Annual*
JAOS	*Journal of the American Oriental Society*
JRAS	*Journal of the Royal Asiatic Society*
JSOTSup	*Journal for the Study of the Old Testament*, Supplement Series
K.	Kouyunjik Collection, British Museum (text collection)
KAI	H. Donner and W. Röllig, *Kanaanäische und aramäische* Inschriften (3 vols.; Wiesbaden: Harrassowitz, 1962–64)
KAR	Erich Ebeling (ed.), *Keilschrifttexte aus Assur religiösen Inhalts* (2 vols.; Leipzig: Walter de Gruyter, 1919 and 1920)
KAT	Kommentar zum Alten Testament
KTU	M. Dietrich, O. Loretz and J. Sanmartín (eds.), *Die keilalphabetischen Texte aus Ugarit* (AOAT, 24; Kevelaer: Butzon and Bercker; Neukirchen–Vluyn: Neukirchener Verlag, 1976)
MIO	*Mitteilungen des Instituts für Orientforschung*
MNB	Monuments de Ninive et de Babylone, Louvre (text collection)
MRS	Mission de Ras Shamra
NorTT	*Norsk Teologisk Tidsskrift*
OrAnt	*Oriens antiquus*
OBO	Orbis biblicus et orientalis
RA	*Revue d'assyriologie et d'archéologie orientale*
REB	Revised English Bible
RivB	*Rivista biblica*
RSP	Loren R. Fischer *et al.* (eds.), *Ras Shamra Parallels* (AnOr, 49–51; Rome: Pontificium Institutum Biblicum, 1972–81)
SJOT	*Scandinavian Journal of the Old Testament*
SWBA	The Social World of Biblical Antiquity Series
TEO I	Pierre Bordreuil, Dennis Pardee, *et al.*, *La trouvaille épigraphique de l'Ougarit*. I. *Concordance* (Ras Shamra-Ougarit, 5; Paris: Editions Recherche sur les civilisations, 1989)
TO I	A. Caquot, M. Sznycer and A. Herdner, *Textes ougaritiques*. I. *Mythes et légendes* (Littératures anciennes du Proche-Orient, 7; Paris: Editions du Cerf, 1974)
TO II	A. Caquot, J.-M. de Tarragon and J.-L. Cunchillos, *Textes ougaritiques*. II. *Textes religieux et rituels: Correspondance* (Littératures anciennes du Proche-Orient, 14; Paris: Editions du Cerf, 1989)

TRU	Paolo Xella, *I testi rituali di Ugarit*. I. *Testi* (Studi semitici, 54; Rome: Consigli Nationale delle Ricerches, 1981)
TuL	Erich Ebeling, *Tod und Leben nach den Vorstellungen der Babylonier* (Berlin & Leipzig: Walter de Gruyter, 1931)
UBL	Ugaritisch-Biblische Literatur
UF	*Ugarit-Forschungen*
Ug	*Ugaritica VI* (MRS, 17; Bibliothèque Archéologique et Historique, 81; Paris: Librairie Orientaliste Paul Geuthner, 1969)
UL	Cyrus H. Gordon, *Ugaritic Literature: A Comprehensive Translation of the Poetic and Prose Texts* (Scripta Pontificii Instituti Biblici, 98; Rome: Pontificium Institutum Biblicum, 1949)
UT	Cyrus H. Gordon, *Ugaritic Textbook* (AnOr, 38; Rome: Pontificium Institutum Biblicum, 1965)
VAT	Tontafelsammlung, Vorderasiatische Abteilung, Berlin Museum (text collection)
VT	*Vetus Testamentum*
VTSup	*Vetus Testamentum*, Supplements
WVDOG	Wissenschaftliche Veröffentlichungen der Deutschen Orient-Gesellschaft
WUS	Joseph Aistleitner, *Wörterbuch der ugaritischen Sprache* (Berichte über die Verhandlungen der sächsischen Akademie der Wissenschaften zu Leipzig, 106.3; Berlin: Akademie Verlag, 1963)
ZA	*Zeitschrift für Assyriologie und Vorderasiatische Archäologie*
ZDPV	*Zeitschrift des deutschen Palästina-Vereins*

INTRODUCTION

In his book *Psalmenstudien II: Das Thronbesteigungsfest Jahwäs und der Ursprung der Eschatologie*, the Norwegian scholar Sigmund Mowinckel presented the theory that in pre-exilic Israel a feast of the enthronement of Yahweh was celebrated. According to Mowinckel, the participants in this cultic event experience how Yahweh fought and overcame the powers of chaos, other gods and hostile peoples. The exodus from Egypt and the wondrous crossing of the Reed Sea is commemorated and re-experienced in the cult. Then Yahweh victoriously enters his temple, seats himself on the throne as king and judges both the peoples and the gods, who are obliged to submit themselves to Yahweh. This judgment, however, renders salvation for Israel.

Further, according to Mowinckel, the enthronement festival of Yahweh was celebrated every year in the autumn and was part of the harvest festival. The coming of Yahweh signifies new creation, rain and fertility, and hence happiness.

Psalmenstudien II was written before the discovery of the cuneiform texts from Ugarit. It was not difficult, however, for Mowinckel and his followers to see these new texts as a confirmation of the hypothesis on the enthronement festival of Yahweh: the Baal-cycle (KTU 1.1; 1.2; 1.3; 1.4; 1.5; 1.6), in this school of thought, was construed as the cult-text for the New Year festival which, or so they held, was once celebrated in Ugarit. The participants of this cult event would have experienced how the fertility god Baal fights the powers of chaos, dies, rises again and seats himself on the throne as king. During the period when Baal is dead the land languishes; as Baal comes to the throne again abundant fertility returns to the land. Thus the Baal-cycle is, according to this school, the cult-text of the enthronement of Baal. This suggestion having been made, it was fairly simple to put forward the hypothesis that the Israelites had taken over this Canaanite cult (an Ugaritic cult automatically being thought of as Canaanite) after the conquest and had adapted it to the worship of Yahweh. At a later stage, elements from the Babylonian New Year festival were possibly added.

The aim of this book is to examine the above-mentioned hypotheses. The Ugaritic Baal-cycle and the Old Testament psalms are key texts in this interpretation; in order to avoid rash conclusions, however, these two groups of texts must be analysed separately and in each case the value of our texts as sources for the history of religion must be carefully assessed.

In short, this book will concentrate on the *Sitz im Leben* of the texts in question. If the Baal-cycle is a cult-text, that is, written in order to be performed in some way or another in the temple of Baal, it is a reasonable assumption that the performance would take place during the New Year festival. But my question is: Is it so obvious that the Baal-cycle is a cult-text?

This book also includes a critique of the method of cultic interpretation—what Mowinckel calls 'the cult functional approach' (Mowinckel 1962: I, xxiii).

Chapter 1

MOWINCKEL'S THEORY OF THE ENTHRONEMENT FESTIVAL OF YAHWEH

Mowinckel's theory of the enthronement festival of Yahweh takes its point of departure in a small group of thematically related psalms, that is, Psalms 47, 93 and 95–100. In these psalms Yahweh is depicted as a mighty king who reigns over the entire world (47.3, 8, 9, 10). He subdues foreign nations under Israel (47.4). Israel rejoices, sings and bows down before Yahweh (95.1, 2, 6; 97.8) and so do the nations (47.2, 7, 8; 97.1; 98.4-6; 99.3; 100.1-2). The peoples enter the courts of Yahweh with songs of praise and offerings and prostrate themselves before him (96.7-9). With joyous song and the sound of a shofar, Yahweh ascends (47.6). He seats himself on his holy throne (47.9), the throne that was established long ago (93.2). An important expression in these descriptions is יהוה מָלַךְ (93.1; 96.10; 97.1; 99.1) or מָלַךְ אֱלֹהִים (47.9). Mowinckel translated this expression as 'Yahweh has become king'.

The situation depicted in these psalms is very similar to the ceremony of the enthronement of an earthly king: The prince on his horse is accompanied by a ceremonious procession to the place of the anointment. A priest anoints the new king and places the crown on his head. The king is escorted to the assembled people, who hail him and clap their hands while the trumpets and other instruments resound (cf. the description of an enthronement in 1 Kgs 1.32-40 and 2 Kgs 11.12). The king is cheered with a 'Long live the king!' (יחי המלך—1 Sam. 10.24; 2 Kgs 11.12), perhaps with the mention of the king's name: 'Long live King Adoni'jah!' (1 Kgs 1.25) or 'Long live King Solomon!' (1 Kgs 1.39). On two occasions, however, we find the expression 'מָלַךְ NN' (NN has become king), namely, מָלַךְ אבשלום בחברון (Absalom has become king in Hebron; 2 Sam. 15.10) and מָלַךְ יהוא (Jehu has become king; 2 Kgs 9.13), which is rather similar to the expression יהוה מָלַךְ (Yahweh has become king) mentioned above.

According to the Masoretes, מָלַךְ is to be construed as a verb in the
perfect tense and not as part of a nominal clause (i.e. as מֶלֶךְ—king),
'which would no doubt be the most likely interpretation of the conso-
nantal text to come to mind, because of the rare occurrence of the verb
mālakh [to be or become king], as well as from the point of view of any
unreflecting dogmatism' (Mowinckel 1962: II, 222 n. 6). According to
Mowinckel, Hebrew verbs have at the same time an ingressive as well
as a durative meaning. מָלַךְ thus means 'to be king' and 'to become
king'; the emphasis, however, is on the ingressive aspect 'to become
king'. The expression 'מָלַךְ NN' is a hail to a king at his enthronement.
מָלַךְ can be translated either way; the ingressive aspect is in focus (the
prince is about to become a king) but the durative aspect is implied: NN
has become king and shall therefore reign hereafter.

The above-mentioned group of psalms (Pss. 47, 93, 95–100) thus
depict the enthronement of Yahweh. This event contains the same elements as the enthronement of an earthly king. There are differences,
however. For instance, Yahweh is not anointed—naturally enough,
since as Yahweh in no way submits himself to the priests. Furthermore
there are some elements in the description of the enthronement of
Yahweh that are not known from the enthronement ceremony of an
earthly king. For example, Yahweh is king of the gods (95.3; 96.4;
97.7) who must prostrate themselves to him (97.7). Yahweh is equally
lord of the sea (93.3-4), which is also forced to honour him (98.7-8).[1]
The notion of creation is likewise found in this group of psalms
(100.3). Yahweh's dominion over the world is based on his creation of
the world (95.5; 96.5). Extraordinary phenomena of nature (e.g. earth-
quakes; 99.1) take place at Yahweh's enthronement (97.2-5).

Mowinckel has grouped together all these elements in a number of
myths that the festival of Yahweh's enthronement is supposed to have
contained: *The myth of creation and the fight with the dragon or primaeval ocean*, which relates how Yahweh created the world and sub-
dued the powers of chaos; *the myth about the combat of the gods*,
which ends with Yahweh judging the gods; *the exodus myth*, com-
memorating the crossing of the Reed Sea; and other myths. All this
works salvation for Israel (Mowinckel 1922: 45-80).

---

1.   The floods, the great waters and the sea (יָם, מִם רבים, נהרות; 93.3-4) are
presumably power(s) of chaos which Yahweh subdues (cf. Pss. 65.8; 74.13; 89.10;
104.6-9; 114.3-5) just as Baal fights *ym*, the god of the sea, in the Ugaritic Baal-
cycle.

The theme of this group of psalms is thus the inauguration of the kingship of Yahweh: Yahweh comes as king, subdues the powers of chaos and the enemies, seats himself on his throne, receives the acclamation of the peoples and establishes his dominion over the world. Among all the peoples in the world, Israel retains a special place.

How is this corpus of psalms to be interpreted? In Mowinckel's day three schools of interpretation were dominant: (1) The historical interpretation; (2) the eschatological or messianic interpretation; and (3) Mowinckel's own solution: the cultic interpretation.

(1) *The historical interpretation*. Those who adhere to this school of thought have tried to find elements in these psalms that link them with concrete historical events. The criticism that has been raised against this historical interpretation is, of course, that the so-called 'enthronement psalms', like the Old Testament psalms altogether, contain very little historical information, if any. For this reason there has been nothing to stop the creative urges of various scholars, and all sorts of historical events from the time of David to the Maccabees have been connected with the psalms.

(2) *The eschatological or messianic interpretation.*[2] According to Gunkel, the emergence of eschatological ideas is to be understood against the backdrop of Israel's misery: the suppression of the country by other peoples, discord among the people, social misery, spiritual poverty and the threats of polytheism have nourished hope of salvation; hope that Yahweh will gather his people together and bring them back home; hope also that Yahweh will rebuild Jerusalem and his temple and subsequently judge the peoples and the wicked; hope that he will reside

---

2.   The words eschatological, prophetic and messianic have often been applied almost synonymously. Eschatology refers to the complex of ideas concerning the end of the world. An eschatological psalm is therefore a psalm which expresses a belief in a new world order after the end of the present world. The psalm may even contain a description of the crucial events at the end of times (apocalyptic). An element of this could be the coming of the Messiah, but not necessarily. A psalm may very well be eschatological without being messianic. According to Gunkel, there is no expectation of a Messiah present anywhere in the psalms. The king who appears in some of the psalms is the ruling king; the eschatological royal power belongs entirely to Yahweh (Gunkel 1913b: 128-29). By 'prophetic psalm'—again following Gunkel—a psalm that in content and form is related to the prophetic works is meant (Gunkel 1933: 329). A psalm can thus contain eschatological elements without being prophetical. Further clarification of the terms can be gained in Lipiński 1962: 156-57 and Wanke 1970.

in the sanctuary and bestow world supremacy upon Israel (Gunkel 1913b: 125).

Eschatological elements are found, according to Gunkel, in a number of psalms. The content of the eschatological hope is that *the time is near*, the time of great miracles, the time of Yahweh's coming. The judgment of Yahweh entails salvation for Israel. The reaction of the people corresponds to Yahweh's actions and is described with various words and expressions of great joy and jubilation (Gunkel 1933: 329-33).

This eschatological hope can be expressed in a more concrete way. Gunkel mentions seven aspects of this hope (following *4 Ezra* 7.91):

(1)   The re-establishing of Jerusalem and the people of Israel.

(2)   The annihilation of the power of foreign peoples.

(3)   The introduction of a new world order after the natural disasters of the end time. These disasters are only implied through hints in the Old Testament psalms, such as through the roar of the sea in Ps. 65.8.

(4)   Before the completion of the new world order Yahweh has to force back the attacking enemies. It is not said *expressis verbis* in the psalms who the attacking peoples are, but it is clear from the context that it is Jerusalem that is under attack. The final battle is to take place in front of the walls of Jerusalem. The motif of *the attacking enemies* is combined with the twin notions of Yahweh as warrior and judge.

(5)   Following the battles of the last times Yahweh assumes royal power. He judges the world in his justice (Ps. 96.13) and makes an end to wars (Ps. 46.10). The reign of Yahweh does not entail an equality of status among all the peoples of the world. Israel takes absolute precedence over the peoples of the earth (Ps. 47.4).

(6)   The temple at Zion is at the centre of the eschatological events. Yahweh has chosen this particular sanctuary above all other sanctuaries. Yahweh seats himself on his throne in the temple and receives homage from Israel and even from the foreign nations (Ps. 47.2).

(7)   The gods in the heavens are to be judged just like the peoples of the earth. Such a judgment can be found in Psalm 82. Here we are told that the gods will have to die just like human

beings. They must prostrate themselves to him (Ps. 97.7; Gunkel 1933: 333-44).

The most severe criticism of the eschatological interpretation has been philological in nature. Quite a few of the eschatological elements mentioned above are expressed in the perfect tense in the psalms, among others the expression יהוה מָלָךְ (Yahweh has become king). Therefore it seems that the psalms refer to past events, not to an eschatological future. The adherents of the eschatological interpretation claim, however, that these perfect tenses belong to a particular category, a *prophetic perfect*. The eschatological events make such an impression on the psalmist that he chooses to express them as something which has already taken place. Mowinckel sensibly objects: 'The poet would then apparently be speaking of the present, whereas in reality he means the future...but this is not implied by so much as a single word' (Mowinckel 1922: 16).[3]

Another objection to the eschatological interpretation is that the psalms do not contain the characteristics of prophecy: 'They [i.e. the psalms] have nothing of prophetic style about them, it is never suggested by prophetic introductory formulas that here we are dealing with prophecies; no trace of the prophetic self-consciousness, such as even a hint of ecstatic vision of future affairs, reveals itself. In short, they are not prophecies' (Mowinckel 1922: 15; cf. Lipiński 1962: 176-77).[4] Prophetic style consists in such expressions as יום יהוה and ביום ההוא or בימים ההם ('the day of Yahweh', 'on that day', 'in these days'), expressions that we do not find in the psalms.[5] יום יהוה, according to Mowinckel, is rooted in the pre-exilic cult: 'The Day of Yahweh is the Day of the Enthronement' (Mowinckel 1922: 230).[6]

In reply to this, the adherents of the eschatological interpretation

---

3. 'Der Dichter spreche dann anscheinend von der Gengenwart, in Wirklichkeit meine er aber die Zukunft...das ist aber mit keinem Worte angedeutet.'

4. 'Sie [i.e. die Psalmen] haben tatsächlich nichts von dem prophetischen Stil, nie wird durch prophetische Einleitungsformeln angedeutet, daß hier etwa Prophetien vorlägen; nie verrät sich eine Spur von dem prophetischen Selbstbewußtsein, wie eine Andeutung von extatischem Schauen der künftigen Dinge. Kurz, Prophetien sind sie nicht.'

5. Except in Ps. 146.4, where the words ביום ההוא ('on that day') cannot reasonably be interpreted eschatologically.

6. 'Der Tag Jahwä's ist der Thronbesteigungstag'. Concerning Mowinckel's views on יום יהוה, cf. Jeppesen 1988.

claim that eschatological psalms are not prophetic psalms. The author(s) of the psalms has/have obviously taken over certain eschatological ideas from the prophets but not 'im vollem Umfange' (to the full extent; Gunkel 1933: 360). Gunkel clearly acknowledges that a number of elements in the eschatology of the prophets are not contained in the psalms. He concludes: 'It is not the eschatology of the great prophets of woe, but only that of the prophets of weal, with their light message, favourable to Israel, that has found its echo in the psalmic poetry' (Gunkel 1933: 361).[7]

Mowinckel also regards the rise of eschatological hopes as the result of historical events. However, he holds that the *contents* of the eschatology must have been derived from the cult. The motifs of the enthronement festival of Yahweh (the subjection of the enemies, the judgment on the peoples, etc.) were projected into the future (Mowinckel 1922: 226-27). This development in the history of religion (the origin of Israelite eschatology) is the subject of the second part of Mowinckel's *Psalmenstudien II*.

(3) *The cultic interpretation*. Mowinckel's alternative to the schools of interpretation mentioned above is the *cultic* principle of interpretation. The adherents of the above-mentioned schools have not—according to Mowinckel—understood the cultic character of the psalms. They are mired in the prejudices about the cult of the Old Testament prophets and modern Protestantism. The result of this has been that they have not been able to find the *Sitz im Leben* of the psalms, even though this is quite obvious: the majority of the Old Testament psalms are cultic psalms composed to be performed in the temple of Jerusalem (Mowinckel 1922: 16-18).

Mowinckel was very much influenced by Gunkel's *gattungs-geschichtliche* (genre-critical) research. Mowinckel intended his theses to be a natural development and correction of Gunkel's *gattungs-geschichtliche* point of view. According to Mowinckel, Gunkel has not taken his own point of view to its logical conclusion (Mowinckel 1962: I, 29). Furthermore, Mowinckel was inspired by the Danish historian of religion Vilhelm Grönbech. Mowinckel took over the notion of the cult as a creative drama from Grönbech and made it the key to the correct understanding of the Old Testament psalms.

---

7.   '...nicht die Eschatologie der großen Unheilspropheten, sondern nur die der Heilspropheten mit ihrer lichten, Israel freundlichen Botschaft hat in der Psalmen-dichtung Widerhall gefunden.'

According to Mowinckel, cult was to the ancient Israelites—and to primitive man in general—a phenomenon that included sacred actions through which society took a share in the divine force, the blessing. The blessing is allotted to the entire community. The individual person only receives a share in the blessing insofar as he or she is part of the community. Thus the members of the community keep covenant with each other. In order to get a share of the blessing the entire community has to covenant with the deity. Therefore the god is lord of the covenant.

To primitive man this is something real. 'To him, it was a fact of experience that he left the cult a different man than when he went to it. He had literally discovered new powers in himself, sensed its remarkable wave motion in his soul' (Mowinckel 1922: 19-20).[8] In the cult he experiences ecstasy—he becomes one with the divine, ἔνθεος (literally 'inspired').

When entering into the cult one enters a sacred world. It would be wrong to say that what takes place is a drama—for the sacred acts that the so-called drama consists of comprise reality for the participants. Primitive man does not distinguish between *sein* (being) and *schein* (appearance). The contents of the dramas are the mythical and historical events on which the existence of the community is based. Each time these events are enacted in the cult they become reality again. In that sense one can say that the cultic drama is a creative or even creating drama. The salvation acts of the past become real here and now.

The basic acts of salvation and the covenant need to be renewed regularly in order that they do not lose their power. This is the reason for the regular cycle in which the covenant is renewed year after year.[9]

This is the cultic conceptual framework in which Mowinckel places the Old Testament psalms, including the so-called enthronement psalms. Mowinckel presupposes that these psalms are cult texts. That means that they must have had a certain place in the cultic drama and that they were related to a particular salvific event which was

8. 'Das ist ihm Erfahrungstatsache, daß er von dem Kulte als ein anderer Mensch geht, als er dorthin ging. Er hat buchstäblich die neuen Kräfte in sich empfunden, ihre seltsamen Wallungen in seiner Seele gespürt.'

9. Concerning the cultic point of view as an interpretive principle in Old Testament scholarship, cf. Mowinckel 1924a, Mowinckel 1922: 16-43 (on which the summary given above is based), Mowinckel 1950, Mowinckel 1962: I, 23-41 and Lipiński 1962: 184-91.

celebrated in the cult. The mythical event to which Psalms 47, 93 and 95–100 refer is the enthronement of Yahweh. Since—from the point of view of primitive man—creative drama makes the event real, present and existing in the here and now, an eschatological interpretation would be wrong. One might conclude, however, that when the enthronement of Yahweh was celebrated in the cult it must necessarily have been a regularly celebrated event (cf. the presuppositions of the cultic principle of interpretation). And since the cultic cycle was identical with the seasonal cycle, the enthronement festival of Yahweh must have been celebrated once a year at a fixed time of year (Mowinckel 1922: 38. He gives no reasons why the presumed cultic cycle must necessarily have followed a one-year cycle. It could equally well have followed a seven-year cycle).

Mowinckel presents yet another argument on behalf of the claim that the enthronement of Yahweh must have been celebrated in the cult. The idea of Yahweh as a king is a characteristic feature of the Old Testament conception of deity.[10] In Samuel's valedictory speech the view is presented that the mere wish for a king is an apostasy (1 Sam. 12). Since the idea of Yahweh was so widespread, it must have been presented in a more concrete way in the cult. Now the fact that Yahweh became king must have been told. And since cult—according to the theory—consists of the repetition and reliving of the fundamental salvific acts, Yahweh's enthronement must have been celebrated in the cult (Mowinckel 1922: 39).

A third argument is based on the parallels from other ancient oriental cultures, in particular the enthronement of Horus in Egypt and, of even greater significance, the enthronement of Marduk in Babylonian religion, as we know it from the Mesopotamian epic *Enuma Elish*.[11]

Enuma Elish was recited on the fourth day of the Babylonian New Year festival, the *Akītu* festival, according to the ritual text which describes it (*ANET*, 331-34). The celebration of Marduk as king in the

10. Mowinckel specifically mentions the following passages where the idea of Yahweh as king is particularly prominent: Deut. 33.4; Isa. 6.5; 33.17, 22; 43.15; 44.6; Jer. 48.15; Mic. 4.7, Pss. 5.3, 44.5; 74.12.

11. It is often said that *Enuma Elish* is an epic of creation. It might be more appropriate to call it an epic poem in the honour of Marduk. This is also what the last line of the fragmentary ending points to: '...the song of Marduk, [Who] vanquished Ti[amat] and achieved the kingship' (cf. A.K. Grayson [trans.], *ANET*, 503).

myth corresponds—according to Mowinckel—to the rituals of the New Year festival (Mowinckel 1922: 40-41).[12]

Mowinckel makes it clear to his readers that the enthronement festival of Yahweh was celebrated annually in Israel during the period of the Israelite and Judaean monarchies. The question is now at what time of the year this festival was celebrated. The Israelite New Year festival in the autumn is a good guess. This festival contains the features that one would expect of such an enthronement festival: New Year's Day is 'holy to Yahweh' (Neh. 8.10); New Year's Day has the characteristic blowing of the shofar which we also find in the enthronement psalms; the Babylonian analogy (the enthronement of Marduk) also points to the New Year festival; at the consecration of the temple in the seventh month the priests bring the ark into the temple (according to Mowinckel, the ark may have been used as a 'stand-in' for Yahweh during the enthronement festival); the rabbinical tradition combines readings for the New Year festival that concern the blowing of the shofar, the kingship of Yahweh, creation, and so forth (Mowinckel 1922: 42-43, 81-89).

Taking his point of departure in the relatively small group of 'actual' enthronement psalms (Pss. 47, 93 and 95–100) and the assumption of an enthronement festival of Yahweh, Mowinckel expands his theory so that it encompasses a great number of psalms (1922: 3-5). These psalms all contain themes that Mowinckel maintains were connected to the enthronement of Yahweh. The enthronement must, for instance, have been introduced by a procession, just as Solomon and the priests went in a procession with the ark at the consecration of the temple (1 Kgs 8) and just as the participants in the Babylonian New Year festival went in a procession to the 'chamber of destiny'. According to Mowinckel, such a procession to the temple seems to have been the cultic background for Psalms 24, 48, 84, 118 and 132, and some of these psalms describe Yahweh as king. Now, since Psalm 132 (with the headline שיר המעלות, 'a song of the ascents') belongs to the cultic text-corpus of Yahweh's enthronement, it is tempting to regard all the other psalms that have the same headline, such as Psalms 120–134, as belonging to the same corpus of songs of the ascents that were sung during the ascent to the temple in the enthronement festival of Yahweh.

---

12. The contention that there is a close relationship between myth and ritual in the Babylonian New Year festival will be dealt with in detail in Chapter 6 of this book.

Secondly, Psalm 24 has a parallel in Psalm 15 and, as Psalm 24 belongs to the extended group of enthronement psalms, then Psalm 15 must do so as well. Thirdly, all the peoples of the earth prostrating themselves to Yahweh is a feature we know from the 'actual' enthronement psalms (Pss. 47, 93 and 95–100); since we find this feature also in Psalm 66a (vv. 1-12), Mowinckel concludes that this particular psalm was also sung at the enthronement festival of Yahweh.

Fourthly, the enthronement psalms relate that Yahweh has come and that he now resides in his city. That is also the subject of Ps. 46.6 and Psalm 76. Fifthly, Mowinckel assigned Psalm 48 to the enthronement psalms because it mentions a festival procession. As a hymn of Zion this psalm has its parallel in Psalm 87. Sixthly, the kingship of Yahweh means judgment over the peoples (Ps. 75), over the gods (Ps. 82) and over Israel (Ps. 50). Psalm 81 has its parallel in Psalm 95. Psalm 8 contains in its superscription the same liturgical expression (עַל־הַגִּתִּית—'al-haggittith', meaning unknown) as we find in Psalm 84. Furthermore, Psalm 8 is a hymn which praises creation, a motif which is also part of the corpus of enthronement texts.

Finally, we find other elements from the enthronement festival (e.g. Yahweh as king, creator, judge or saviour) in Psalms 29, 33, 114 and 149 and in Exod. 15.1-18. A number of psalms that do not directly contain the idea of Yahweh's kingship, among them Psalms 65, 67 and 85, belong to the New Year festival as psalms of harvest and fertility. In Psalm 65, the idea of Yahweh as a fertility god is combined with the notion of Yahweh as creator; in Psalm 67, the idea of Yahweh judging the peoples is juxtaposed with an expression of gratitude over the harvest.

Thus, apart from the eight 'actual' enthronement psalms Mowinckel includes Psalms 8, 15, 24, 29, 33, 46, 48, 50, 65, 66a, 67, 75, 76, 81, 82, 84, 85, 87, 118, 120–134, 149 and Exod. 15.1-18 in this category. Later, Mowinckel added Psalm 68 to the group of enthronement psalms (cf. Mowinckel 1953a).

In short, Mowinckel's theory is that during the monarchy Yahweh's enthronement was celebrated once a year in connection with the New Year festival, which was also a harvest festival. The above-mentioned psalms are cultic texts that were used in this connection. The festival opened with a grand procession in which Yahweh (perhaps as a statue, or represented by the ark, or perhaps invisible) ascended to the temple. The participants in the cultic drama in the temple experience how

Yahweh fights and subdues the powers of chaos, the other gods and the hostile peoples. The exodus from Egypt and the wondrous crossing of the Reed Sea is commemorated (or rather, *experienced*, since what happens in the drama is perceived by the participants as reality). Yahweh victoriously enters his sanctuary, assumes kingship, seats himself on his throne and judges the peoples and the gods. They all have to submit to Yahweh. This judgment entails salvation for Israel. The coming of Yahweh also means re-creation, new rain and fertility.

Chapter 2

A CRITICAL EVALUATION OF MOWINCKEL'S THEORY
ABOUT AN ENTHRONEMENT FESTIVAL OF YAHWEH

Mowinckel's *Psalmenstudien II* has had an enormous influence on later psalm research. A great number of scholars have more or less accepted the hypothesis of the famous Norwegian scholar.

Mowinckel's theory has, of course, also encountered serious opposition;[1] for example, from Gunkel. Gunkel's main objection to Mowinckel's hypothesis is first and foremost 'that he [Mowinckel] was not rigorous enough in his selection of psalms that belong to this festival' (Gunkel 1933: 104).[2]

According to Gunkel, Mowinckel included in his enthusiasm far too many psalms under the designation 'psalms of the enthronement festival of Yahweh'. The implication is that, for Mowinckel, the enthronement festival had become a 'magnet', which attracted too many psalms (Gunkel 1933: 101). Since this festival, of which Gunkel cautiously recognizes the existence, is not directly mentioned in the Old Testament, we can only speak about it from conjectures. 'In addition is the fact that the references which are provided us in such festal poems are usually very indefinite...' This opens the gate to error, a difficulty which the two scholars [i.e. Mowinckel and H. Schmidt] do not seem to have realized with sufficient clarity' (Gunkel 1933: 105-106).[3]

Gunkel advises that in deciding which psalms actually do belong to the category of enthronement psalms, one has to proceed with extreme

1. A survey of the history of research concerning the critics of Mowinckel can be found in Lipiński 1962: 241-72.
2. 'daß er [Mowinckel] bei der Zusammenstellung der zu diesem Fest gehörigen Psalmen nicht streng genug verfahren ist'.
3. 'Dazu kommt noch, daß die Anspielungen, die uns in solchen Festgedichten gegeben werden, ziemlich unbestimmt zu sein pflegen... Dadurch ist nun freilich dem Irrtum Tor und Tür geöffnet, eine Schwierigkeit, die sich die beiden Forscher [i.e. Mowinckel und H. Schmidt] wohl nicht genügend klar gemacht haben.'

caution. Since the hypothetical enthronement festival is characterized by (1) Yahweh becoming king and (2) his entering into his sanctuary and seating himself on his throne, only psalms which contain these two elements may legitimately be regarded as psalms of the enthronement festival of Yahweh. Other psalms may only be taken into consideration if compelling reasons can be adduced (Gunkel 1933: 101).

It is obvious that if one follows Gunkel's very careful suggestions not very many enthronement festival psalms will remain. Gunkel himself concludes that not more than six psalms can reasonably be construed as belonging to this category of psalms, namely Psalms 47, 93, 96, 97, 98 and 99 (Gunkel 1933: 102-108).

Thus Gunkel apparently accepts a modified version of Mowinckel's hypothesis. In actual fact, it is only the *number* of psalms which separates Gunkel and Mowinckel. The basic and structuring ideas in Mowinckel's grand hypothesis are accepted by Gunkel. This is clearly seen in, for example, the following statements by Gunkel concerning the enthronement psalms:

> (a) The enthronement poems were performed in Jerusalem on New Year's Day in celebration of the enthronement of Yahweh; this according to S. Mowinckel and H. Schmidt.
> (b) This celebration presumably arose in the latter days of the monarchy in imitation of and as a counterpart to the Babylonian New Year festival.
> (c) In the practices used in this celebration, as well as in the ideas that were connected with it, the celebration of the enthronement of the worldly king, which had so often been experienced, also became the model (Gunkel 1933: 111).[4]

Gunkel's objections to Mowinckel's theory are apt and adequate. The enthronement festival of Yahweh is not attested in the Old Testament except perhaps in the psalms. Mowinckel responded to such objections with some irritation: 'In response to a misunderstanding that has often been raised by the critics of the festival that has been delineated there [i.e. in Mowinckel 1922] I should like to repeat for the *n*th time a point

4.   'a) Die Thronbesteigungsgedichte sind in Jerusalem am Neujahrstage zur Feier der Thronfahrt Jahves aufgeführt worden; dies nach S. Mowinckel und H. Schmidt. b) Diese Feier ist wohl als Nachahmung und Gegenstück des babylonischen Neujahrsfestes in der späteren Königszeit entstanden... c) Bei den Bräuchen dieses Festes aber und bei den Gedanken, die man damit verbunden hat, wird die Feier der Thronbesteigung des weltlichen Königs, wie man sie so oft erlebt hatte, zugleich Vorbild gewesen sein.'

that is clearly readable in *Psalmenstudien II*, namely that it is not a
matter of "a new festival that is not attested in the sources", but of an
aspect which has been observed either very little or not at all of the
well-known and well-attested autumnal New Year festival, the Festival
of Booths' (Mowinckel 1961: unpaginated Preface).[5] But even this
aspect of the New Year festival is not attested in the sources. It remains
a hypothesis.

Similar hypotheses, albeit with a different content, can easily be
made if one is prepared to do a little juggling with the Old Testament.[6]
Actually, the so-called enthronement psalms can be regarded as a kind
of empty frame in which one can place material of various kinds. If one
combines the historical narrative of Exodus 15 with Psalms 47, 96 or
97, these constructions, these new psalms, will appear surprisingly
'genuine'. And vice versa, if one extracts the hymnic verses of Exodus
15 and combines them all together, the outcome will closely resemble
an enthronement psalm. A similar process can be done with Psalms
135, 118 and 68.

What is the implication of this in regard to Mowinckel's theory? First
and foremost, it demonstrates that the enthronement festival of Yahweh
is nothing but a hypothesis—one possible explanation among many
other hypotheses. The so-called enthronement psalms can be used as a
framework to contain almost any historical, legendary or mythological
narrative. Mowinckel's theory about the enthronement festival of
Yahweh is certainly a magnificent attempt of reconstruction. *His theory, however, is unnecessary.* The so-called enthronement psalms are of
such a character that various festivals with other mythological or
'historical' themes could be claimed to have been the *Sitz im Leben* for
a number of these psalms—even if such hypotheses might not be as
impressive as Mowinckel's.

Other objections than the one mentioned above can be raised to
Mowinckel's hypothesis. For instance, Mowinckel conjectures that the

5.   'Gegen ein von den Kritikern häufig geäussertes Missverständnis des dort
[i.e. in Mowinckel 1922] gezeichneten Festes, wiederhole ich hier zum xten Mal,
was schon in *PsSt II* klar zu lesen steht, dass es sich nicht um ein "neues in den
Quellen nicht bezeugtes Fest", sondern um ein bis da sehr wenig oder gar nicht
beachtetes Aspekt des wohlbekannten und wohlbezeugten Herbst- und Neujahrsfestes, des Laubhüttenfestes, handelt.'

6.   The following is a concentrated summary of Rendtorff 1959 ('The Victory
Hymn in Exodus 15 and its Relation to the Enthronement Psalms'; translation
mine).

enthronement of the king was celebrated in Judah on New Year's Day in the same way as in Babylon: that is, the king's accession to the throne was celebrated as an annual event during which the king would go through a ceremonial re-installation. Mowinckel bases this hypothesis on Jeremiah 26:

> If a great festival was celebrated 'at the beginning of the reign of Jehoiakim' in Judah in the Babylonian period, in which it was a matter of course that all the people were gathered together (Jer. 26.1ff.), then the assumption is inviting that they also celebrated in Judah the actual enthronement at the same time as in Babylon, namely on New Year's Day; for [Hebrew] *rēšip mamlāchäp* [the beginning of the reign of…] is linguistically precisely the same as [Akkadian] *rêš šarrûti* (Mowinckel 1922: 7-8).[7]

It is obvious that Mowinckel is skating on thin ice here, as there is no reason to believe that the many people from the 'cities of Judah who come to worship in the temple of Yahweh' (Jer. 26.2) come in order to celebrate an enthronement festival or the like. It is not even said that they have arrived on the occasion of the beginning of the reign of Jehoiakim. בראשית ממלכות ('At the beginning of the reign of…') is simply an indication of time just as the similar expression in Jer. 27.1.[8]

Mowinckel stresses the importance of Marduk's enthronement during the *Akītu* festival in Babylon. But even this enthronement is but a hypothesis created on the basis of the mention of Marduk's enthronement in the so-called epic of creation, *Enuma Elish*. According to the ritual text of the *Akītu* festival, *Enuma Elish* is to be recited and no more than that. There is no mentioning of ritual actions in that connection (cf. Chapter 6 below).

The conclusive objection that one has to make against the cultic

---

7. 'Wenn nun in Juda in babylonischer Zeit ein großes Fest *bᵉrēšíp mamlächäp Jåhūjåqīm* gefeiert wurde, bei dem es als selbstverständlich vorausgesetzt wird, daß alles Volk versammelt ist (Jer. 26,1ff.), so liegt die Annahme sehr nahe, daß man auch in Juda die eigentliche Thronbesteigung zu der selben Zeit wie in Babylonien, d.h. am Neujahrstage, feierte; denn *rēšíp mamlächäp* ist sprachlich genau dasselbe wie *rêš šarrûti*.'

8. According to Mowinckel, בראשית ממלכת is a designation for an inaugural period of a new king's reign in the deceased king's year of death, the period between the deceased king's day of death and the following New Year's Day. In Babylonian this period is called *rêš šarrûti*. On New Year's Day, after the enthronement, the new king's first year of reign began. (Cf. Michelet, Mowinckel and Messel 1929–63: II, 305.)

method of interpretation is, however, that this method determines the result of the examination beforehand. When one has decided and made part and parcel of one's theory the idea that the fundamental acts of salvation must be represented dramatically in the cult at regular intervals, it then becomes obvious that the central theme of a certain group of psalms must have been represented dramatically.

Let us try to put the cultic principle of interpretation to the test. Creation is one of the themes of the enthronement psalms and creation is obviously part of the basic acts of salvation. Thus creation must have been celebrated in the cult at regular intervals, probably once a year. Genesis 1 was probably the cult legend of this festival, since myth (and Gen. 1 is undeniably myth) is but a projection into primaeval times of what is enacted in the cult. All this we can say with a high degree of certainty, following the principles of cultic interpretation. Moreover, it is quite likely that the duration of this festival was one week (cf. Gen. 1). The assumption that Genesis 1 was a cult-text tallies perfectly with our knowledge of other Near Eastern cultures in antiquity. After all, *Enuma Elish*—the Babylonian cult legend of the New Year festival—is itself a creation epic!

Just as we are able to reconstruct to some extent the contents of the enthronement festival of Yahweh from the cult-texts—the enthronement psalms—we are also able to reconstruct the celebration of creation from the text of Genesis 1. The congregation was obviously gathered together at the beginning of the annual week of celebration in a 'vast and dark waste', that is, the temple (microcosmos). The king would represent God. (We remember, of course, that to the participants of the cultic drama everything that takes place in the drama is real!) Precisely how it was presented that רוח אלהים מרחפת על־פני המים ('the spirit' or 'Wind of God swept over the face of the waters') cannot be known. We can, however, with some certainty assume that the sea of cast metal mentioned in 1 Kgs 7.23-26 would have been used in this connection. The cultic connection in the following is much clearer. The king says, 'Let there be light!', and the king, or perhaps a servant, lights a candle, torch or the like. Thus word corresponds to action, myth to rite. Also vv. 14-19 must have been accompanied by similar actions. This is the cultic light that is hinted at in Isa. 9.1. The cultic reality which was well known to people is here applied eschatologically, in the same way that the themes of the enthronement festival of Yahweh are reinterpreted eschatologically (cf. Mowinckel 1922: 211-324).

The mention of the waters in the following verses (vv. 6-10) must also allude to rites in connection with the above-mentioned sea of cast metal.

We simply do not know how the creation of plants, animals and eventually man was depicted in the cultic drama. In any event, we should not be led to construe the cultic drama as anything similar to modern theatre.

> The dramatic tools could have been very primitive indeed. It is often the case that one does not see the actual actions, or what might look like action by modern conceptions, but symbols, mimetic gestures, all manner of manipulation of symbolic objects which are accompanied by interpretative words, often in poetic form (Mowinckel 1922: 25-26).[9]

One cannot avoid noticing, however, that the Israelite cult of fertility as we know it from Genesis 1 is of a quite different character than its Canaanite opposite number.

The cultic week ends with a day of rest.

The interpretation above of Genesis 1 is, of course, a joke—but a serious joke, meant to illustrate the arbitrariness of the cultic method. The cultic method of interpretation was applied here according to the principles described by Mowinckel. And the above hypothesis (the interpretation of Gen. 1) *is* true if one follows Mowinckel: 'A hypothesis is "true" if it is able satisfactorily and without remainder to explain the facts of a matter' (Mowinckel 1922: 44).[10] If we have now succeeded in explaining Genesis 1 'satisfactorily and without remainder', following the principles of cultic interpretation, we may safely conclude that our hypothesis is true. It is unnecessary to search for another *Sitz im Leben* for the text.

My main objection to the cultic method of interpretation as such (and also to Mowinckel's actual use of these principles in his *Psalmenstudien II*) is that *any text containing mythical elements can be interpreted as a cult-text*. This is the Achilles heel of the cultic principle of interpretation.

9.   'Die dramatischen Mittel können sehr primitiv sein. Sehr häufig sieht man nicht die eigentlichen Handlungen oder was nach modernen Begriffen nach Handlung aussieht, sondern Symbole, mimische Gesten, allerlei Manipulationen mit symbolischen Gegenständen, die von deutenden Worten, häufig in poetischer Form, begleitet werden.'
10.   'Eine Hypothese ist "wahr", wenn sie die vorliegenden Tatsachen befriedigend und restlos zu erklären vermag.'

Chapter 3

THE ENTHRONEMENT FESTIVAL OF YAHWEH
AND THE UGARITIC TEXTS

Psalmenstudien II was written before the discovery of the Ugaritic
texts. Subsequently, however, it was not difficult for Mowinckel to find
support for his theories about the enthronement festival in the Ugaritic
Baal-cycle:[1]

> The conception of the god as king is...older than Israel. But it is not
> only this general form of the idea that Israel has received from the
> Canaanites, it is the same with its cultic and epic expression of the
> enthronement of the god. In the religious texts from the town of Ugarit
> (Ras Shamra) in Phoenicia, the feast of the rains—the harvest and New
> Year festival—signifies the revival and resurrection of the god Baal or
> Aleyan Baal, who, having conquered death (*Môt*), seats himself on the
> throne and is proclaimed king of gods and men. Together with the
> enthronement of the god goes the building and consecration of his
> temple.
>   These performances were apparently common to the whole of
> Canaan, and not restricted to Ugarit. That they have been of importance
> for the development of the cult of Yahweh in Jerusalem cannot be
> doubted (Mowinckel 1962: I, 132).

Mowinckel himself did not find any reason (or time?) to perform a
more systematic study of the Ugaritic texts. He regarded the pre-
Ugaritic and post-Ugaritic psalm research (at least on European
ground) as a continuum.[2] The Ugaritic texts would at the most prompt a
'Frühdatierung' (early date) of the enthronement psalms.[3]

---

1.   The more important Ugaritic texts can be found in English translation in,
e.g., Gibson 1978 and in French translation in *TO* I and *TO* II.
2.   The European psalm research contrasted to some degree the American, cf.
Mowinckel 1955b.
3.   Cf. Mowinckel's short remark on this in Mowinckel 1961: unpaginated
Preface.

On the other hand, Mowinckel's successor, Arvid S. Kapelrud, devoted much of his energy and time to studying the Ugaritic texts (Kapelrud 1940, 1952, 1963 and 1969). He identified the hypothetical Ugaritic New Year festival with its Canaanite counterpart. 'The character of this festival as it was celebrated at Ugarit (*and correspondingly in Canaan*) is clearly indicated by what we are told about Baal' (Kapelrud 1963: 67-68; emphasis mine). Kapelrud held that we possess a direct testimony to this festival in the Ugaritic texts, even if these texts might not be completely identical with the texts that served in the cult (Kapelrud 1963: 67).

> The texts about Baal were the liturgy of the festival. Baal's conflicts with Prince Sea and with Mot, his descent under the earth and his triumphant return, the building of the temple, the festival of its dedication, and the sacred marriage all took place in the cult in a realistic and vivid presentation which lasted throughout the days when the autumnal New Year Festival was celebrated. The worshippers were active participants in the cult, weeping and lamenting when Baal descended under the earth and joining wholeheartedly in the joyful celebrations when he returned triumphantly after defeating his enemies. The climax came with his enthronement and the great sacrificial feast, at which there was boisterous junketing and the wine flowed free, the whole ending in unrestrained debauchery when the god's marriage was celebrated (Kapelrud 1963: 68).

Having stated this, it is easy for Kapelrud to describe this development from a history of religions point of view:

> When the Israelites settled in the land, they adopted Canaanite practices and the Canaanite cult and related them to Yahweh. Their borrowing included the agricultural autumnal festival. At a later stage features from the Babylonian New Year Festival were added (Kapelrud 1963: 72).

This development in the history of religion presupposes, however, that a New Year festival was indeed celebrated in Ugarit and that the Baal-cycle is the cult-text used in that connection. The plot of the Baal-cycle is supposed—to a greater or lesser degree—to have been enacted in the cult. Furthermore, it is maintained that this hypothetical Ugaritic cult was representative of 'Canaanite' cult in general.

These are the assumptions that I will investigate more closely in the following chapters. Since the Ugaritic Baal-cycle is our only source bearing on the hypothetical Ugaritic New Year festival, a quest for the *Sitz im Leben* of this text will form the point of departure in this investigation.

Chapter 4

INTERPRETATIONS OF THE UGARITIC BAAL-CYCLE

The great epic texts from Ugarit hold a dominant place in descriptions of Ugaritic religion. These epics are often divided into two groups: myths and legends. According to the traditional history of religions terminology, myths are stories about gods, whereas legends are about gods and human beings. While there is some disagreement about the *Sitz im Leben* of the Ugaritic legends, the *aqht-* and *krt-*epics (i.e. as to whether these texts were used in connection with the royal cult or whether they are just examples of early entertaining fiction[1]), the Baal-cycle has far too often been construed as a cult-text in an axiomatic way: scholars have not felt the need to argue for this point of view. The claim has been made that the Baal-cycle was not just recited, rather, it has been maintained that it was the 'libretto'[2] of a cult-drama that was performed in one of the temples of Ugarit (Gaster 1950). Against the backdrop of these suppositions the scholar will paraphrase the mythological texts relatively uncritically; the place of each individual god in the Ugaritic pantheon is established and their individual character is described through their epithets and their role in the myths. Thus, or so it has been held, a paraphrase of the Baal-cycle will provide the basic structures of Ugaritic religion. Having carried out this process, the scholar may include archaeological material in his or her synthesis. A number of depictions of gods (figurines and reliefs) correspond very well to the image that one gets of Baal and El, for example, through reading the texts.[3] On the other hand one may wonder why Ugarit had a

1. Cf. Liverani 1970. In reading the articles of Liverani I have made extensive use of Niels Peter Lemche's translation into Danish (Liverani 1993).
2. The word 'libretto' has vanished from the second edition of *Thespis: Ritual, Myth and Drama in the Ancient Near East* (1961)—but Gaster's basic interpretation is unchanged. Cf. below, pp. 40-52, on Theodor Herzl Gaster.
3. Depictions of Baal and El can be found in Caquot and Sznycer 1980: pls. 7, 8, 9 and 10.

great temple for *dgn*, a god, who does not play any significant role in the epic texts. Furthermore it is remarkable that the ritual texts do not mention any cult drama.

A great many essays on Ugaritic religion thus consist of a relatively uncritical paraphrase of the epic texts (first and foremost the Baal-cycle). What is generally lacking are some initial considerations on the methodological problems involved in a description of Ugaritic religion, the nature of the sources, and the like. Instead, the epic texts are used in an axiomatic way as primary sources for a description of Ugaritic cult and religion.

I do not intend to go through the entire scientific literature on the subject of 'The *Sitz im Leben* of the epic texts from Ugarit'. I have instead chosen a few representative monographs and articles to review. The interpretations that I have chosen to deal with are mainly concerned with the Baal-cycle, as it is above all in this epic that scholars have detected a Ugaritic cult-text.

Flemming Friis Hvidberg, Weeping and Laughter
in the Old Testament

Flemming Friis Hvidberg's famous study was originally published in Danish in 1938; it was posthumously translated into English by Niels Haislund and edited by F. Løkkegaard in 1962. Hvidberg's work is remarkably lacking in argumentation in favour of the view that the Baal-cycle is a cult-text.

On pp. 11-14, the outline, theses and conclusions of the book are presented in the form of a summary. It is said about the texts of the Baal cycle: 'They are cultic texts' (Hvidberg 1962: 13). The arguments for this view are to be found in the chapter entitled 'Function and Fundamental Meaning of the Canaanite Texts' (1962: 50-78). In this chapter we find Hvidberg's reflections on the *Sitz im Leben* of the Baal-cycle. Hvidberg has, of course, only treated those parts of the poem that were accessible to him when he wrote his book (i.e. 1938). He has translated large parts of the Baal-cycle (1962: 22-49).

Hvidberg emphasizes the many dialogues of the text, for example, II AB V 106–VI 35[4] which he describes as 'almost completely full of dialogues' (1962: 50). 'Apart from the short introductory sentences: *wy'n ktr whss*, "and Ktr-w-Hss said" and *wy'n b'l*, "and Aliyn Ba'al said"

---

4. See KTU 1.4 v 44–vi 35.

before the lines, there are no narrative sentences at all in this scene—or at most a single one (lines 109-110)' (1962: 50). A translation of the above-mentioned text shows, however, that Hvidberg isn't right.[5] Below I have translated a part of this text which is obviously narrative in character:

> *y*[tl]k*.llbnn.w'ṣh*
> *l[š]r*yn.mḥmd.arzh*
> 20 *hn*[.l]bnn.w'ṣh*
> *šr*y*n.mḥmd.arzh*
> *tšt*[.]i*št.bbhtm*
> *nb[l]at.bhklm*
> *hn[.]y*m.wtn.tikl*
> 25 *išt[.]bbhtm.nblat*
> *bhkl*m*.tlt.kb'* (read *rb'*) *ym*
> *tikl*[.i]š*t.bbhtm*
> *nblat[.]bhklm*
> *ḫ*mš.t*[d]t*.ym.tikl*
> 30 *išt*[.b]b*htm.nblat*
> *b*[qrb.h]k*lm.mk*
> *bšb'*[.]y*[mm].td.išt*
> *bbhtm.n*[bl]at.bhklm*
> *sb.ksp.lrq*m.ḥrṣ*
> 35 *nsb.llbnt.*[6]

They [we]nt to Lebanon and its trees,
to [S]irion (and its) beautiful cedars;
20 Behold [Le]banon and its trees,
Sirion (and its) beautiful cedars!
A fire is set in the house,
fla[m]es in the palace.
Behold, a day and the second
25 the fire consumes in the house, the flames
in the palace. The third and the fourth day
the [fi]re consumes in the house,
the flames in the palace.
The fifth and the sixth day
30 the fire consumes [in] the house, the flames
[in the middle of the pa]lace. But then,

---

5.   Hvidberg wrote that: 'It is to be hoped that the attempt at a translation used as basis [for the survey of the contents] can be given elsewhere' (Hvidberg 1938: 28), which he, however, never succeeded in. The editor, F. Løkkegaard, presumes that the plan was shelved during the war (Hvidberg 1962: 41 n. 2).
6.   KTU 1.4 vi 18-35.

on the seventh d[ay] the fire is removed
from the house, the f[lam]es from the palace.
They turn silver into plates, gold
35 is turned into bricks.

It is not decisive that Hvidberg has missed the narrative character of this passage, even though it weakens his argumentation. He is aware that there are passages in the Baal-cycle 'which clearly communicate actions' (1962: 50). The crucial thing is that Hvidberg uses the above-mentioned text as an argument for a dubious conclusion: 'This and other passages of a similar kind suggest that we have a dramatic performance before us, a play' (1962: 50). On the contrary! The fact that the Baal-cycle contains obvious (and even poetic) passages of narration such as the one translated above, the fact that the text (as far as we can see) contains a single coherent story which would make sense if recited for an audience without any actions to supplement it, means that we need not place the text in a cultic setting in order to understand it. The cultic *Sitz im Leben* is quite superflous.

Arvid S. Kapelrud, Baal in the Ras Shamra Texts

Arvid S. Kapelrud is one of the scholars who introduces some methodological considerations about the character of the epic texts before interpreting them. Thus he begins his book, *Baal in the Ras Shamra Texts*, with the promising observation that the Ras Shamra texts are to be read in their own context before the relationship between the Ras Shamra texts and the Old Testament can be examined. If not, the result could easily be that the Ugaritic texts are interpreted in the light of the Old Testament and not 'in their own context and meaning' (1952: 11).[7] The goal of Kapelrud's investigation is 'to find out the character of Baal in the R Sh texts and his role' (1952: 11). Kapelrud assures his reader that 'a thorough examination of the texts will form the basis for all conclusions' (1952: 11). The underlying principle of interpretation is the hermeneutical circle: the detail is to be interpreted from the whole and the whole from the detail. Kapelrud furthermore promises to examine the presuppositions with which we encounter the text. This question is to be dealt with 'in some width' (1952: 12).

---

7.   *Baal in the Ras Shamra Texts* was reissued in 1973 in a revised and abridged Norwegian edition (Kapelrud 1973). Kapelrud's main points are, however, unchanged.

However, it is clear from the text that Kapelrud uses the notion of 'pre-suppositions' in a very restricted sense: namely, to denote presup-positions about *what kind of literature the Ugaritic epic texts belong to.* The hermeneutical analysis that Kapelrud promises is thus of a very limited nature.

Kapelrud also wants to include material from other Near Eastern cultures from the second millennium BCE in his comparison with the Ugaritic texts (1952: 12-13). However, he is quite aware of the danger in letting the interpretation of the Ugaritic texts be determined by what we know (or think we know) about other religions or cultures.

The first task Kapelrud tackles is to decide what kind of texts we are dealing with. '"The *Sitz im Leben*" ...has to be made clear before an adequate interpretation is possible' (1952: 12). Kapelrud begins his quest for the *Sitz im Leben* of the epic texts by viewing them from dif-ferent perspectives and by assessing the various genre-assignments that have been accorded to them.

> It is evident that seen from a purely literary point of view the greater part
> of the so-called AB cycle may be called epics... But I cannot see that
> this designation goes further than the purely literary form. We shall have
> to keep an open eye for the form of the texts, but I cannot accept this
> point of view as the most valuable and profitable for our understanding
> of the texts (1952: 14).

Because of the contents of (some of) the epic texts, the term 'myth' has often been applied to these texts. But, according to Kapelrud, even that designation does not help us to obtain a deeper understanding of the texts. 'That designation implies that we have a story concerning super-human beings, but that is also about all. It is thus a term that does not actually say much' (1952: 15).

Kapelrud thinks that we must look at the texts from another perspec-tive in order to understand them. This is precisely where the reader expects Kapelrud to give his contribution to a better understanding of the *Sitz im Leben* of the texts. But it is precisely here that Kapelrud's argumentation stops. Kapelrud postulates that 'our texts are not "l'art pour l'art", they were not told just for the enjoyment of the audience. We are entitled to suppose that they had a certain "place in life"' (1952: 15).

Thus Kapelrud escapes the problem that I find crucial in this connec-tion. Can we say with any kind of certainty or even probability that the Ugaritic epics were part of Ugaritic religious life in the sense that they were used in the cult or otherwise regarded as 'sacred' or 'canonical' writings? Contrary to what Kapelrud has suggested, it makes perfectly good sense to say that reciting texts 'for the enjoyment of the audience' is also a *Sitz im Leben*.

Without any real argumentation, Kapelrud maintains the viewpoint that the Baal-cycle is a cultic text which was used in the temple cult. 'Nobody can doubt that these texts were recited or used for dramatical performances in the temple they mention so frequently' (1952: 18). Note how the idea of 'dramatical performances' is introduced in a quite unsubstantiated way.

Kapelrud makes one digression which might superficially look like some kind of evidence: he mentions the fact that the epic texts from Ugarit were all found in the library of the high priest.

> This building was situated in a dominating place in Ugarit, between the two temples of the town. There can be no doubt about the intimate con-nection between the three. This fact points already to the probability that the texts found in the library will have to be considered as texts intended for use in the temples, as far as concerns the religious texts at least (1952: 17).[8]

Obviously Kapelrud considers the Baal-cycle to have belonged to the group of 'religious texts'.

One problem remains. What is a 'religious text'? Are all texts which contain stories about gods religious texts? The problem is that the find-site is being advanced as evidence that epic texts—of whose *Sitz im Leben* we are wholly ignorant—were used in the cult. That is what Kapelrud does. Or rather, he seems to have determined the *Sitz im Leben* of the text beforehand. The mentioning of the find-site is just another piece of 'evidence'. But taking Kapelrud's argumentation seri-ously one moment: since the find-site is the only piece of evidence he presents, would Kapelrud have concluded that the Baal-cycle was 'told just for the enjoyment of the audience' had the clay tablets on which it is written been found in the palace archives?

If one insists that the find-site of the clay tablets (i.e. the archaeologi-cal context of the tablets) is to be used as an argument in a discussion of the *Sitz im Leben* of the Baal-epic, the result is going to be quite dif-ferent from Kapelrud's conclusion.

It seems as if the clay tablets in the building complex of the high

8.   The two temples are the temples for Baal and *dgn* on the acropolis of Ugarit.

priest were divided according to their contents when they were stored. Ritual-texts (i.e. texts that contain descriptions of how various offerings are to be performed, by whom and when, etc.) were stored in a room in the north-western part of the building complex. This is also where SS (KTU 1.23) was found—a text which contains both mythical and ritual elements. The Baal-cycle and *aqht* and *krt* all seem to have been stored in rooms in the vicinity of the street commonly known as 'Rue de la Bibliothèque'. The reason I present this so cautiously ('It seems as if...') is that data on the precise find-site of a number of tablets are missing. The material that the archaeologists have left us with points in the direction that I have sketched above.[9] In any case, the find-site cannot be of decisive importance when texts are to be interpreted.

We will have to look for the *Sitz im Leben* of the texts—if we can hope to find it at all—in the contents of the texts themselves.[10] Kapelrud devotes most of his book to a textual analysis and interpretation of the Baal-cycle, but he does so with the basic prejudice that the Baal-cycle is a cultic text, a prejudice which is only substantiated through postulates like his claim that the texts are not 'l'art pour l'art'; that is, that they were not told merely for the enjoyment of the audience (1952: 15).

Theodor Herzl Gaster, Thespis: Ritual, Myth and Drama in the Ancient Near East

In terms of the history of research, Gaster's book continues the tradition of Frazer's *The Golden Bough: A Study in Magic and Religion* and the English 'myth and ritual' school.[11] The principles of the 'myth and ritual' school are beautifully applied to the Ugaritic texts in *Thespis*. For that reason, the 'myth and ritual' school as such is not to be discussed further in this chapter. I would simply be repeating the arguments that I use against Gaster.[12]

9. Cf. Chapter 5, where I have dealt exhaustively with this problem.

10. The very best thing would, of course, have been to have another text, a ritual text, for instance, which would describe under what circumstances the Baal-cycle was read—if it was read at all.

11. The major works of this school are Hooke 1933 and 1935.

12. A critique of the 'myth and ritual' school can be found in Frankfort 1951. Hooke's answer to this is in Hooke 1958: 3. Cf. also the critique of the theory of 'ritual pattern' in Bernhardt 1961: 51-66.

According to Gaster, the Baal-cycle is '*a seasonal myth based on the traditional ritual drama of the autumn festival*' (1961: 129; emphasis his). Or, as he puts it more bluntly the first time the Baal-cycle is mentioned in his book: 'The *Poem of Baal* ... s really the cult-myth of the Autumn Festival...' (1961: 47; emphasis his). The argumentation for this is twofold, since the interpretation is based on both 'internal and external grounds' (1961: 129). The internal and external grounds are, however, woven into each other: the text is interpreted with the help of the hypothetical construct called the 'seasonal pattern' (below abbreviated to SP), and thus the Baal-cycle is given a meaning and function it did not necessarily enjoy. Conversely, the Baal-cycle is also used as evidence of the validity of the SP. In the following I shall try to distinguish Gaster's internal and external arguments from one another, and try to pinpoint how his argument falls apart.

The Seasonal Pattern
Gaster's point of departure is that primitive man construes life decidedly differently than we do:

> From the standpoint of a primitive community, life is not so much a progression from cradle to grave as a series of leases annually or periodically renewed and best exemplified in the revolution of the seasons (1961: 23).

This renewal (especially the changes of the seasons) is not so much something that is determined by the laws of nature. Rather, it is something man must fight for. Therefore 'primitive' humans have prepared a number of seasonal rites, 'a regular program of activities... which, performed periodically under communal sanction, will furnish the necessary replenishment of life and vitality' (1961: 23).

These rituals are accompanied by myths, the function of which is to express on an ideal and durative level that which on the real and punctual level is enacted in the cult. According to Gaster, myth is—so to speak—'born' out of ritual: 'Myth is not... a mere outgrowth of ritual... it is the expression of a parallel aspect inherent in them [i.e. in sacral acts] from the beginning' (1961: 24-25).

According to Gaster, rites were originally performed jointly by the entire community. In the course of time the king assumed the cultic functions by representing the entire society. In the cult (which Gaster perceives as the punctual level) the king realized the actions which were performed by the gods in primaeval times (the durative level). The primaeval battle of the gods is the archetype of the drama, which is regularly performed in the cult.

For Gaster, the connection between the punctual and the durative level is *myth*. The amalgamation of myth and ritual is *drama*.

The seasonal rites are performed according to a specific pattern, the 'seasonal pattern', which consists of four elements: *mortification* (various forms of fasting and other kinds of abstinence); *purgation* (cleansing); *invigoration* (strengthening of the 'good forces'); and *jubilation*. Gaster finds examples of these elements from all over the world and from all times. Against this background Gaster creates a 'typical seasonal ceremony' which is a highly hypothetical construction. Gaster himself admits that there is hardly a single instance in which all the elements of the SP are extant (1961: 61).

The hypothetical construct SP, which I have briefly presented above, is based on vast material from all times and from all over the world. The main problem in Gaster's book is the way he uses the material. The question we shall have to raise is whether Gaster is sufficiently aware of the character of his material and whether his interpretation is adequate.

Gaster presents an overwhelming amount of examples of rites and folklore drawn from various cultures and from all times. Gaster emphasizes in the preface to the second edition that he does not presuppose any direct connection between the examples. 'The comparison is on the psychological, not the historical level' (1961: 13).[13] And yet he uses the *psychological* parallels that he thinks to find in ancient Near Eastern, Egyptian, Greek and Roman rituals and in popular customs from all over the world (Peru, Siam, Russia, Togoland, New Guinea and Japan, to mention but a few) to reconstruct (or rather, construct) a SP. The SP is thus a hypothetical construct based on religious phenomena drawn from all over the world. The only thing these phenomena have in common is that they seem to stem from the same psychological experience. Gaster admits that the image that he produces of 'a typical seasonal ceremony' is 'synthetic'. However, he continues: 'Nevertheless, its typical and representative character is guaranteed by the fact that each of them is indeed widespread and not confined to any one particular culture' (1961: 61). On the contrary! The 'original' ritual that Gaster

---

13. This important statement is not in the first edition of the book (Gaster 1950). Gaster has, however, not taken it to its logical conclusion—that would have meant rewriting the book!

has constructed and presented in his book is not typical simply because 'all the elements rarely survive together in any single instance' (1961: 61). Even one of the rare examples of a complete 'Seasonal Ritual'—namely, the ritual of the Babylonian *Akītu* festival—is incomplete according to Gaster. Gaster forces his construct into the ritual (cf. below, pp. 44-48).

It is now possible to answer the question that I posed above. In the preface to the second edition (and only there), Gaster presents a reasonable understanding of the character of his vast material, which is that the parallels to the great many rites and customs he refers to may stem from the same psychological experience: the changes of the seasons may have been experienced as a combat, the result of which is of great importance for mankind. What the very many examples have in common is to be found on the psychological level. Gaster is thus apparently aware of the character of the material; he does not, however, draw the appropriate consequences from this knowledge. An analysis that should have been kept on the psychological level is used by Gaster to construct 'a typical seasonal ceremony' on the 'concrete' level. Gaster's application of the material cannot be said to be adequate.

A critique of this sort could be raised against the whole idea of the 'ritual pattern'. As Bernhardt puts it:

> One now explains the transmitted points of agreement between the religions and cultures of the ancient Near East not only through one and the same primaeval human situation; one attempts to determine the latter in detail and speaks of the migration of a 'ritual pattern', that is, one moves from a religio-psychological effort into the realm of concrete historical relationships (1961: 55).[14]

Quite ironically, Gaster himself brings a beautiful example of how correspondence in one field should not be transferred to another, and the example is from the world of philology. Both in Indo-European and Semitic languages we find the term 'head' in the meaning 'the source of a river'. A comparison on the psychological level would here be in order. But philologically, ראש has nothing to do with κεφαλή or *caput*

---

14. 'Man erklärt nämlich nun die ermittelten Übereinstimmungen in den Religionen und Kulturen des Alten Vorderen Orients nicht nur durch die gleiche menschliche Ursituation und sucht diese wiederum ihrerseits noch näher zu bestimmen, sondern redet von einer Wanderung des "ritual pattern", wechselt also vom religions-psychologischen Ansatz über in den Bereich konkreter historischer Beziehungen.'

(Hebrew, Greek and Latin for 'head' and 'source of a river'; Gaster 1961: 13). The analogy on the psychological level in this example has no equivalent on the philological level. Gaster should have been equally rigorous in his work on folklore. One may note various psychological correspondences in religious ideas and practices all over the world. But an analysis of this should be kept on the psychological level. Consequently one cannot assume—as Gaster does—that many of the rites and customs mentioned in his book are necessarily rooted in a cultic seasonal ritual.

It is true that the changing of the seasons is of major importance for human beings and that human beings all over the world have anticipated the coming of the rain (or of the sun) with some anxiety. This is a fundamental condition for life on earth and human beings have always given expression to this in various ways. Cultic rites may be one expression, the fight between two persons disguised as summer and winter another (Gaster 1961: 37), and a third one may take the form of stories in which the leading characters are construed as representatives of the antagonists of the SP. These different expressions may not have anything to do with each other except on the psychological level. As mentioned previously, Gaster should have kept to the psychological level—which in fact the preface to his second edition presupposes—rather than postulating that various popular traditions and works of literature from all over the world are rooted in 'certain traditional patterns of ritual' (1961: 12).

In short, through a careless application of vast and varied material, Gaster has constructed an artificial pattern, known as the 'seasonal pattern'. This is the Procrustean bed in which the same material is placed.

The Seasonal Pattern and the Akītu *Festival*

One of the few, but nevertheless very important, examples Gaster thinks to have found of a complete seasonal pattern ritual is the Babylonian *Akītu* festival (1961: 62-64). The ritual is, however, only a complete seasonal ritual because Gaster reads his own construction, the SP, into the ritual.

Gaster himself points to the fact that it is doubtful whether the appointment of an interim king (*interrex*) is an element present in the ritual (1961: 69 n. 4). Gaster postulates that during the *Akītu* festival 'a sacred pantomime in which the god was portrayed as having sunk into the netherworld and was ritually bewailed' took place (1961: 64).

'Subsequently, of course, he returned to earth' (1961: 64). There is no evidence for such a pantomime. Gaster refers in this connection to S. Langdon's very questionable interpretation of VAT 9555 (Langdon 1923). Langdon sums up VAT 9555 under the headline 'The Death and Resurrection of Bêl-Marduk' and he interprets the text as a cult-commentary to a now lost ritual of the Babylonian New Year festival.

The evidence for a mimetic combat which represents the struggle between the divine protagonists is remarkably scarce. Gaster concludes by referring to a text and a seal impression that there once existed such a 'mimetic combat'. The text is the very enigmatic VAT 9555. The main character in the text, the god Bel, is kept prisoner, and two other gods—one of them being Nabu—are looking for him. The proceedings of a (perhaps) divine sitting of a court are mentioned, a mourning procession is described, *Enuma Elish* (the Babylonian so-called 'myth of creation') is recited to Bel, prayers are recited, and there is a race. It is related that the chariot for the New Year temple (*bet Akītu*) is empty and that combats are taking place in the town and in the temple. Finally, a curse is pronounced over anyone who might destroy the tablet, and readers of the text are urged to pass on the message of the text.[15]

The mimetic combat is supposedly attested in lines 23 and 69 which run:

23   [*ur-ki*] *ša* ^dEN *àna ḫur-sa-an il-lik-u-ni* URU *àna* UGU[-*šú*] *it-ta-bal-kàt qa-ra-bu ina* ŠÀ *u*[-*pu*]-*šú*

23   [When] Bel had gone to *ḫursan*, the city rebelled against him; they fight in it.

69   *šu-nu ḫu-ur-ra-a-te ina* ŠÀ ^{giš}IG *up-ta-li-šú qa-ra-bu ina lìb-bi up-pu-šú*

69   They made holes in the door; they fight in it [i.e. the temple-building].[16]

15. VAT 9555 = KAR no. 143. This text exists in two versions: the longer, so-called Assur Version, which I follow here; and a Niniveh Version. Transcription and translation of the text together with a commentary can be found in von Soden 1955, and in Frymer-Kensky 1983. There is a brief summary in Pallis 1926: 252-53. Livingstone 1989 presents a fresh reading based on new collations of the originals. This is probably the edition to refer to for years to come, but unfortunately it came to my attention too late to be thoroughly incorporated into my manuscript.

16. Notes on transliteration and translation: In Labat's *Manuel d'épigraphie akkadienne* the particular form of the sign *ša* that we find in this text is missing (Labat 1976: 163 sign no. 353). I find it hard to see that there should be enough

In short, there is no basis in this text for concluding that a 'mimetic combat' was part of the ritual of the *Akītu* festival. Furthermore, the question must be raised whether VAT 9555 has anything to do with the *Akītu* festival at all. Von Soden says decidedly no:

> What is announced here concerning Bel is so extraordinary that it can hardly have been part of the cult legend of the Babylonian New Year festival, or of some other festival for Bel-Marduk. All cult legends glorify their deity, even though this might be only in the mode of *per aspera ad astra*. Here, however, there is really no trace of any glorification of Bel; rather, the deity appears in a somewhat disreputable role as an accused. No Babylonian myth offers similar treatment to any of the great gods. They speak of similar fates only in connection with demons, or with forces of the primaeval world, such as Tiamat and her followers (von Soden 1955: 161).[17]

In terms of form, VAT 9555 shares many characteristics with the so-called cult-commentaries, as for instance TuL 7, 8 and 10. Cult-commentaries are characterized by the way they interpret 'hymnic expressions, cultic acts, and the employment of particular objects in cult-mythological...in which connection the priestly authors very often grant very free rein to their imaginations' (von Soden 1955: 157).[18]

space at the end of line 23 for the two signs *up* and *pu*, as generally suggested (von Soden 1955: 134; Frymer-Kensky 1983: 133; Livingstone 1989: 83). Compare with line 69, in which the scribe has had more space.

ḫursan may mean—apart from 'Flußordalstätte'—simply 'mountain' (cf. von Soden 1955: 141. Cf. also *ḫuršanu* A and *ḫuršanu* B in *CAD*, VI, 253-55 and *ḫursanu(m)* II/*ḫuršanu* II and *ḫuršanu* I in *AHw*, 359-60. Both dictionaries list the quotation mentioned above with the meaning 'ordeal'. In *CAD* the word in our context is simply 'translated' 'the place of the *ḫ.*-ordeal' [*CAD*, VI, 254-55]). Frymer-Kensky understands *ḫursan* as a placename (1983: 138-39). I have chosen not to translate the word since the exact meaning is not of great importance for our purposes.

17. 'Das, was hier von Bel berichtet wird, ist so ungewöhnlich, daß es in der Kultlegende des Neujahrsfestes in Babylon oder eines anderen Festes für Bel-Marduk keinesfalls gestanden haben kann. Alle Kultlegenden verherrlichen ihren Gott, mag es auch *per aspera ad astra* gegangen sein. Hier ist aber von einer Verherrlichung Bels wirklich nichts zu finden, sondern der Gott erscheint in einer recht kläglichen Rolle als Angeklagter. Kein babylonischer Mythus weiß von einer ähnlichen Behandlung eines der großen Götter zu berichten; sie erzählen ähnliche Schicksale nur von Dämonen oder den Urweltmächten wie Tiamat und ihrem Gefolge.'

18. 'hymnische Aussagen, Kulthandlungen und den Gebrauch bestimmter

While cult-commentaries as such are intended for priests alone (thus TuL 7 forbids its readers to reveal its contents to non-initiates) the colophon of VAT 9555 curses anyone who does not disseminate the contents of the text.[19] Because of this—and after a thorough analysis that I will not summarize here—von Soden characterizes VAT 9555 as a 'propagandistic work aimed at a wide public' (1955: 157).[20] According to von Soden, the text represents an attempt to give a religious legitimation to Senacherib's devastation of Babylon and the temple of Marduk in the year 689 BCE (cf. von Soden 1955: 161-66).

According to Frymer-Kensky, however, this text was used in connection with the return to Babylon of the statue of Marduk in 669:

> It seems likely that the text justifies and celebrates, not the subjugation of Marduk, but his ultimate vindication after his tribulations. The events that prompted the creation of the text would then be, not the destruction of Babylon in 689, but the return of the statue of Marduk to Babylon in 669 (1983: 132).

I shall not venture to present a new interpretation of VAT 9555 here. The interpretation mentioned above suffices to show that the text is so complicated that one cannot conclude from a rather casual mention of warlike actions that a 'mock combat' was necessarily part of the ritual of the *Akītu* festival.

In order to substantiate his interpretation, Gaster refers to a cylinder seal published by Langdon in *The Illustrated London News*. The impression on the seal shows a number of masked people apparently fighting each other. Langdon dates the seal to c. 3000 BCE (1928: 991).[21] There is nothing to suggest that this has anything to do with the *Akītu* festival. S. Smith, whom Gaster also refers to in this connection (Gaster 1961: 69 n. 7), does not offer any arguments that Gaster does not also employ—he merely expresses his wish that he would later be able to prove that 'there was a fight of the gods, and a slaughter of certain underworld gods' (S. Smith 1928: 867 n. 1).

The proof—or even a vague suggestion—that a 'mimetic combat' was part of the ritual of the *Akītu* festival is almost non-existent. Gaster

Gegenstände im Kult mythologisch..., wobei die priesterlichen Verfasser ihre Fantasie oft sehr weit schweifen lassen'.

19. VAT 9555, lines 70-76 (= *KAR*, I, 234 [no. 143 rev.], lines 19-25).
20. 'für die breite Öffentlichkeit bestimmtes Propagandawerk'.
21. The seal-impression is also published in the official excavation report, namely, Langdon 1924: IV, pl. 34 n. 3.

presumes, however, that there was a sort of weakened form of ritual combats, namely 'ceremonial races'. Such a 'race' is—according to Gaster—attested in VAT 9555 lines 7-9, where one or more persons are running around in the streets looking for Bel (1961: 69 n. 7a). The conclusion that this scene is a 'ceremonial race' that, of course, is rooted in a 'mimetic combat', is preposterous. If the hypothesis of a race is to be brought into the argument it would have been a lot more obvious to refer to the race (*lismu*), which is mentioned *expressis verbis* in line 57![22]

The Development of Myth

Gaster presupposes, as we have seen, that myth corresponds to ritual. Myth transfers or 'translates' the punctual contents of ritual to the durative level. The task of the scholar is to re-translate from the durative to the punctual level.

Myths are to a very high degree only extant in a form separated from the cult. During the Babylonian *Akītu* festival, *Enuma Elish* is *recited* (cf. Chapter 6 of this book). Gaster writes that VAT 9555 and a similar text, K. 3476,[23] 'are but learned lucubrations, and the interpretations which they propound can be regarded only as the product of scholarly ingenuity'. Gaster continues, however: 'Nonetheless, they help us to recover details of the ritual and show how, even on this level of academic exegesis, the basic interrelation of rite and myth was clearly apprehended' (1961: 90). It does not occur to Gaster at all that the reason that we know of cult-commentaries like VAT 9555 exclusively in this 'academic' form is perhaps that the close and unspoiled relation between myth and ritual has only very rarely existed and may not be 'original'.

However, as we have seen, Gaster presupposes an intimate connection between cult and myth: 'Myth is not...a mere outgrowth of ritual...it is the expression of a parallel aspect inherent in them [i.e. sacral acts] from the beginning' (1961: 24-25). Gaster explains the form in which we often find myths, that is, as mythical narratives separated from the cult, to be the result of urban culture:

> With the growth of urban life, however, new conceptions emerge, and
> the processes of nature are no longer considered so dependent upon the

22. VAT 9538 rev. (= *KAR* no. 219 rev.) line 10. This text is a duplicate of VAT 9555, what H. Zimmern has already pointed out (Zimmern 1918: 3 n. 1).
23. K. 3476 can be found in Pallis 1926: pls. 5-7.

operations of men. When that happens, the traditional ceremonies lose their urgency and tend to survive not on account of any functional efficacy but solely by reason of their wider mythological significance and of their purely artistic appeal (1961: 83).

Gaster is only able to see this development away from cult as degeneration: 'It is an essential part of my thesis that the genre underwent normal artistic evolution (or degeneration) and ended up, as often as not, as a mere literary convention' (1961: 13). Gaster thus allows himself to view the creation of literature as a deplorable development; this view is due to a sentimental understanding of Near Eastern man in Antiquity. According to this way of thinking, correspondence between myth and ritual (or said in a more prosaic way: between word and action) is the natural, unspoiled, original state of things. Individual phrases and scenes in the myth must necessarily have had their counterpart in concrete actions in the cult. Narrative in which words are separated from actions is a later development compared to the earliest ideal times—and thus represents degeneration. I will expound on this rather romantic view in Chapter 7.

The Seasonal Pattern and the Baal-cycle
On the surface, the Baal-cycle is a fascinating story about the quarrels of various gods and goddesses. According to Gaster, however, it has a deeper meaning: 'In reality, *it is a nature myth and its theme is the alternation of the seasons*' (1961: 124; emphasis his). The key to this interpretation is to be found in the names of the protagonists: *ym*, *mt* and Baal.

Baal is the rain- and thundergod. We know this from his epithets and from other things said about him in the Baal-cycle.[24] His nature is also underlined by the fact that one of his daughters is called *ṭly*, 'nymph of the dew' (Hebrew טל; Ugaritic *ṭl*, dew), and another daughter of his is called *arṣy*, 'nymph of the earth'. *ym* is the god of the sea, as is equally evident from the etymology of the name (Hebrew ם; Aramaic ימא). *mt* is the god of death. *mt* means 'death' in a number of semitic languages.

Thus Baal, *ym* and *mt* each has his own dominion. Their internal struggles and their changing control over the earth may be interpreted as the changing of the seasons in the Syrian area. In the rainy season

---

24. Examples of this can be found in Gaster 1961: 124-25. Concerning Gaster's translation of II AB IV 68 (= KTU 1.4 v 6): 'he "appoints the due seasons of his rains"'. Cf. pp. 67-71 on Dirk Kinet below.

(from the end of September to the beginning of May), Baal rules, but
not until he has defeated *ym*, who in the beginning of this season threat-
ens with floods and equinoctial gales.

Gaster goes so far as to call the Baal-cycle 'an allegory of the seasons' (1961: 126). This method of interpreting that involves a 'translation' of each individual unit of the narrative into meteorological
phenomena is highly problematical. The following is an example of just
how difficult it is to make the Baal-cycle fit a seasonal Procrustean bed:
Gaster places the short-term rule of *ym* and the combat between Baal
and *ym* at the beginning of the rainy season:

> Baal, as genius of the rainfall, holds sway during the wet season, from
> late September until early May. But he does so only after curbing and
> subduing Yam, the rival power of the waters which, at the beginning of
> that season, threaten to overwhelm the earth with floods and equinoctial
> gales and thereby to 'possess' it (1961: 126).

In favour of his interpretation Gaster refers to a paragraph in
G. Dalman's *Arbeit und Sitte in Palästina*, the heading of which reads:
'Gewitter, Schnee, Hagel und Hochwasser *im Frühling*' (emphasis
mine; Dalman 1928: I, 304-308, esp. 307-308). Johannes C. de Moor,
on the contrary, places the rule of *ym* in the winter and the struggle
between Baal and *ym* in the end of the winter: KTU 1.2 i (in de Moor's
terminology: III:i with the heading 'Ba'lu is handed over to Yammu'),
takes place during the winter, whereas KTU 1.2 iv (de Moor: III:iv,
'Yammu is defeated by Ba'lu, there is heat for the stalks sprouting in
the fields') takes place at the end of winter.[25]

To say that the Baal-cycle is an allegory of the seasons is in itself
problematical. As Gaster says, 'But the poem is more than a mere literary allegory of the seasons' (1961: 128); and he ends his analysis of
the Baal-cycle by concluding that the poem ('both its structure and its
sequence') corresponds exactly to the 'ritual pattern'—the pattern that
he has constructed himself. It is in this way that Gaster reaches the conclusion that I cited at the beginning of this section: '*On both internal
and external grounds, therefore, there is every reason for seeing in the
Canaanite Poem of Baal a seasonal myth based on the traditional
ritual drama of the autumn festival*' (1961: 129; emphasis his).

25. De Moor has developped the allegorical interpretation *in absurdum* in de
Moor 1971 and *ARTU*. Cyrus H. Gordon had already warned against the seasonal
interpretation in *UL*, 3-5. A critique of de Moor 1971 can be found in Margalit
1980: 204 n. 2, and in M.S. Smith 1986: 314-16.

Gaster's Conclusions

Gaster's conclusions are as unclear as his method is questionable. How are we to construe 'our texts'? What is Gaster's point? This is clear in the first edition where the bold statement is made:

> Thus...we reach the inescapable conclusion that *our Ancient Near Eastern Texts are indeed the libretti (or, at least, the residual forms) of seasonal pantomimes and thus the prototypes of classical Greek and modern European Drama* (1950: 72; emphasis his).

This conclusion corresponds to the preface to the first edition of *Thespis: Ritual, Myth and Drama*, in which Gaster calls the texts in question 'traditional "books of words" of religious ceremonies'. These texts are only fully understood 'if read against the background of the rituals which they accompanied' (1950: ix).

There is, however, a vast difference between the viewpoints presented by Gaster in the first edition and in the preface of the second edition: 'It is not argued that the texts themselves were actually the libretti of liturgical dramas or the spoken accompaniments of ritual acts' (1961: 12). If this were to be the fundamental viewpoint of the second edition, one should have expected an entirely new book from Gaster's hand. This is, however, not the case. Gaster is far from having drawn the consequences of the sentence quoted above. The idea of actual enactment of the texts permeates the book in spite of the preface. The word 'libretto' has—as far as I have been able to see—disappeared from the second edition. Thus the sentence '...*our Ancient Near Eastern Texts are indeed the libretti...*' has vanished from the second edition. The organization of the material and the references have been made clearer, but the fundamental viewpoint is unchanged: 'It is thus once again apparent that our texts were designed for recitation or enactment in connection with temple ceremonies. In other words, they were part of an established order of service rather than mere specimens of literary creativity' (Gaster 1961: 102 [1950: 71]). The preface has been changed; the book is otherwise unaltered.

An Analogical Experiment

The Danish writer Ebbe Kløvedal Reich once said 'There are two main ways of thinking. You may call them the logical way and the analogical way, the scientific and the poetical. Logic has to do with obvious differences, analogy with hidden similarities' (Reich 1986: 28; translation mine).

Thespis: Ritual, Myth and Drama may well be regarded as 'an analogical experiment'.[26] Viewed from this perspective, Gaster's book is
most inspiring and worth reading.

André Caquot, 'Problèmes d'histoire religieuse'

Caquot begins his article with a sharp delimitation of his material: it is
only possible to describe a religion on the basis of *texts*.

> In the absence of all contemporary written evidence, the religious inter-
> pretation of architectural remains or of sculpted monuments remains too
> arbitrary for the historian to make such use to any significant extent
> when attempting to reconstitute something of a dead religion (1969:
> 61).[27]

Even if Caquot's delimitation of the material may seem a bit too sharp
(from the existence of cult-objects and from temples one can conclude
that there was a cult—perhaps one could be so precise as to say that it
was a sacrificial cult—and maybe one could get some kind of impression of the various religious conceptions in the religion in question), he
is nevertheless right if we are considering more than a superficial
description of the practices of the religion.

The discovery of private and official libraries in Ugarit has finally
provided us with such texts as are needed for a more detailed description of a West-semitic religion in the second millennium BCE. But we
should not believe that we have thus found evidence for a West-semitic
religion as such in the Bronze Age; this is Caquot's second restriction
(1969: 62). We do not know what roles or functions various gods may
have had in other city-states, even though the names of the Ugaritic
gods may be found elsewhere in the Near East.

In this connection Caquot mentions a study by K.-H. Bernhardt
(Bernhardt 1967), which shows how the attributes allotted to the goddess Ashera differ so much in Ugarit and Israel respectively that one
cannot—except for the similarity of names and the fact that they are
both goddesses—speak of any actual relationship between the two.

---

26. This expression stems from Kløvedal Reich; he uses it to describe his book
Frederik: En folkebog om N.F.S. Grundtvigs tid og liv (Reich 1986: 28).

27. 'En l'absence de toute donnée écrite contemporaine, l'interprétation religieuse de vestiges architecturaux ou de monuments figurés demeure trop aléatoire
pour que l'historien puisse en tirer parti quand il essaie de reconstituer quelque
chose d'une religion morte.'

Bernhardt admits, however, that precisely because of the similarity of names one could speak of a connection between the Ugaritic *aṯrt* and the Old Testament Ashera but no more than that. 'The two goddesses have nothing to do with one another' is Bernhardt's conclusion (1967: 174).[28]

It may be justified to speak of a certain amount of particularism: each city worshipped its own gods. On the other hand, it is equally clear that from the Ugaritic scribe Elimilku to the authors of the Old Testament, the people of the Syro–Palestinian area have had a common cultural and religious heritage that we can detect in parallel words and expressions in Ugaritic and Hebrew literature.[29]

After these initial methodological considerations Caquot turns to 'the outstanding work of Ugaritic literature' (1969: 67),[30] which is to say, the Baal-cycle, which he characterizes as 'an agrarian myth' (1969: 69).[31] Baal is lord (*b'l*) of rain and storm. In order to water and fertilize the earth, the rain has to leave heaven and make its way to the earth, which in the myth is illustrated through Baal's going to the subterranean abode of *mt*, Death. Quite understandably Baal hesitates to 'give himself' ('faire le don de sa personne'), that is, to pour out the life-giving water. In the narrative this is expressed through Baal's refusal to open a window in his palace.

Water does not stay in the earth for ever. It evaporates, goes up into the air and forms clouds which yield rain anew. In this process the goddesses *'nt* and *špš* play a decisive role: *'nt* personifies the sources (*'n* means 'source') that feed on the subterranean water, and *špš* (the sun) who brings about the necessary evaporation.

But myth is more than that, Caquot maintains: 'The myth of Ba'al is more than the story of a "spot of water", more than a "scientific" explanation of the cycle of water vapour. It is more than a narrative intended to charm and instruct' (1969: 69).[32] In less than ten lines Caquot presents the hypothesis that the Baal-cycle was recited annually at an

---

28. 'Die beiden Göttinnen haben nichts miteinander zu tun.'
29. Cf. *RSP* on Ugaritic–Hebrew parallels.
30. 'la pièce de choix de la littérature ougaritique'.
31. 'un mythe agraire'.
32. 'Le mythe de Ba'al est plus que "l'histoire d'une goutte d'eau", plus qu'une explication "scientifique" du cycle de l'humidité. C'est plus qu'un récit destiné à charmer ou à instruire.'

autumn festival, a very similar hypothesis to Mowinckel's reconstruction of the Israelite New Year festival. Caquot does not advance any evidence to substantiate his hypothesis.

On the other hand, however, Caquot also seeks to delimitate the importance of the Baal-cycle. Caquot is quite aware that the Baal-cycle is not a creation of the ordinary man, but sees it rather as a sophisticated work of scribes: that is, of the intellectuals (1969: 70). Apart from this we know of a slightly different pantheon from the ritual texts than the one we know from the mythological texts (Caquot 1969: 73-74). With these facts in mind Caquot writes: 'It is possible that we only possess this mythology in some sort of official variant that was peculiar to the priests of Ba'al' (1969: 74).[33] It is very important to keep this qualification in mind when interpreting the Baal-cycle, even if it could be expressed more pointedly: perhaps what we encounter in the Baal-cycle was really only representative of a single person (perhaps Elimilku). I shall enlarge somewhat on this idea presently.

Caquot tries, however, to describe what he calls 'la piété ougaritique' ('the Ugarit piety'):

> One [the inhabitants of Ugarit] expects of the gods the good things in life, fertility, fecundity, health, the maintenance of the cosmic balance...they require of the deity, no matter what his name might happen to be, salvation and blessing, protection and favour (1969: 74).[34]

But, as Caquot says himself, this religious attitude is not the exclusive property of Ugaritians; rather, 'it is almost a constant of semitic religious behaviour, in the first millennium as well as in the second' (1969: 74).[35] This is how general a description of Ugaritic religion has necessarily to be, if one wants to avoid extreme and unsupported hypotheses.

As Caquot writes in his concluding remarks: 'The ambitions of the

33. 'Peut-être ne saisissons-nous que la mythologie en quelque sorte officielle du clergé de Ba'al.'

34. 'On [= les ougaritains] attend des dieux les bienfaits da la vie, la fertilité, la fécondité, la santé, le maintien de l'équilibre cosmique...ils demandent à la divinité, quelque soit son nom, salut et bénédiction, protection et faveur.' Cunchillos has reached more or less the same conclusion on the piety of the Ugaritians from statements in Ugaritic letters (Cunchillos 1984 and 1985).

35. 'c'est presque une constante de la religiosité sémitique, au Ier millénaire comme au second'.

historian of religion who concerns himself with the area we have been dealing with should remain modest' (1969: 75).[36]

Hartmut Gese, Die Religionen Altsyriens

In the book entitled *Die Religionen Altsyriens, Altarabiens und der Mandäer* (Gese, Höfner and Rudolph 1970), Hartmut Gese wrote the part on 'Die Religionen Altsyriens' ('The Religions of Ancient Syria'). The material is overwhelming and may be divided in two main groups: (1) the archaeological remains (temples and other cult-sites, cultic artifacts, depictions of deities, etc.); and (2) the very large number of texts from the middle and late Bronze Age. Gese writes about the first group of material (the non-written sources): 'The expressive potential of these materials is naturally extremely limited' (Gese 1970: 21);[37] although he thinks that the iconographic representations possess a higher value as sources.

A description of religion in Syria in the second millennium BCE will have to be based to a very large degree on written sources, and in this connection the Ugaritic texts play the leading role. Apart from the fact that an entire chapter is dedicated to 'The Ugaritic Mythic–Epical tradition' (1970: 50-93)[38] it is striking that the framework of Gese's reconstruction of the Syrian pantheon in the chapter 'The World of the Syrian Deities in the 2nd Millennium BCE' (1970: 94-172) consists of the epic texts from Ugarit. Each individual god is characterized according to the role he or she holds in the mythical texts; extra-Ugaritic texts and non-written material are used to complement the picture that the Ugaritic texts give.

In his description of the sources for a description of Syrian religion,[39] Gese distinguishes—as is often done in Ugaritic studies—between

36. 'Les ambitions de l'historien des religions qui s'intéresse au domaine dont nous traitions doivent demeurer modestes.'
37. 'Natürlich ist die Aussagekraft dieses Materials durchaus begrenzt.'
38. 'Die mytisch-epische Überlieferung Ugarits'.
39. 'Die Quellen zur syrischen Religion' (Gese 1970: 21-35). Notice the singular form: 'Die Quellen *zur syrischen Religion*' (my emphasis). Considering the dominating place the Ugaritic material holds in the description it is understandable that Gese writes 'religion' in the singular. It is, however, a 'bad' point of departure to postulate one common religion in Syria in the second millennium BCE. Gese does not do that in other parts of his presentation. Therefore he should have stuck to the expression 'die Religionen Altsyriens' here.

large and small texts: the large texts are the myths and epics, the small
ones are 'Hymns, liturgies, rituals...conjurations, god-lists, and records
of the temple administration' (1970: 26).[40] By virtue of this distinction
SS (KTU 1.23) is counted among the larger texts, whereas KTU 1.100,
which is in fact a few lines longer, is counted among the small texts.
The distinction between large and small texts is thus to some extent
more a question of the nature of the text than a question of quantity.

Gese admits that because of the character of the source material it is
not possible to present a comprehensive description of religious life in
Ugarit in the late Bronze Age. 'The Ugaritic mythical traditions are by
far the most informative source, although they are encumbered by a
number of peculiar philological difficulties' (1970: 37).[41] In my opin-
ion, it is not so much the philological difficulties that present the main
problem, when the texts are to be used as a basis for a description of
Ugaritic religon; it is, rather, the fact that we do not know the status of
the texts in antiquity, their *Sitz im Leben*.

According to Gese, these texts offer the best picture of the religious
world of Ugarit, partly because they present a more complete impression of a pantheon, and partly because they 'have their expressive value
as recital-texts...in the function of their proclamation' (1970: 50).[42]
Concerning the first issue—namely, that the great Ugaritic texts present
a 'closed and extensive picture...which presupposes inner coherence'
(1970: 50)[43]—Gese is, of course, right. In particular, the Baal-cycle is
one great narrative with a plot, inner coherence and a detailed character
sketch. The second issue—namely, that the great texts are 'Rezitationstexte', 'recital texts'—is also a reasonable assumption. It is not unlikely
that the texts were recited on one or another occasion. However, an
extraordinary, perhaps somewhat enigmatic, relative clause has been
added by Gese to his term 'recital texts', where he qualifies these as
texts 'which as such have their expressive value in the function of their

40. 'Hymnen, Liturgien, Ritualen...Beschwörungen, Götterlisten und Urkun-
den der Tempelverwaltung.'
41. 'Am weitesten führen uns noch die ugaritischen mythischen Über-
lieferungen, die allerdings mit besonderen philologischen Schwierigkeiten belastet
sind...'
42. 'Rezitationstexte,...in der Funktion ihrer Verkündigung, ihren Aussagewert
haben.'
43. 'in sich abgeschlossene Gebilde größeren Umfangs..., die einen inneren
Zusammenhang voraussetzen'.

proclamation' (1970: 50).[44] Now the term 'proclamation' ('Verkündi-gung') is a theological notion which fits very badly in this connection. Gese should at least have defined what he means by 'proclamation', since this term denotes something more than the simple recital of a text. Gese has certainly not brought us nearer to a definition of the *Sitz im Leben* of the epic texts from Ugarit in a convincing way.

However, Gese is well aware that because of the character of the source material it is impossible to give a thorough description of Ugaritic religion. He mentions that in the ritual texts a number of gods are enumerated that we do not find in the epic texts, just as archaeologists have unearthed a vast temple for *dgn*, a god, who does not hold an important role in the mythical texts. He remarks that 'Even apart from such differences one must fundamentally be aware that the epic tradition represents a special element in religious life; it is not a mirror of the entire world of religious conceptions' (1970: 50).[45]

Gese thus prepares the reader for a not very ambitious interpretation of the Baal-cycle. His analysis of the Baal-cycle is about 28 pages long. He expounds on its inner narrative coherence, the sequence of tablets and various possible translations. Extra-Ugaritic material (Hebrew, Egyptian and Akkadian texts, etc.) are adduced for comparison. In his analysis, Gese does not go into very much detail about the possible relationship between the texts and the cult.

Towards the end of Gese's analysis of the Baal-cycle there is, how-ever, a break in his way of arguing. Here he seems to admit that 'the individual elements in the narrative largely seem to be of a ritual nature' (1970: 79),[46] a statement for which there is absolutely no evidence in the Ugaritic texts. Not even in Gese's own analysis of the Baal-cycle is there anywhere presented the idea that individual scenes, let alone the entire epic, may have been enacted in a cultic connection.

In Gese's analysis there are a few scattered thoughts about the relationship between texts and cult, but none of these considerations justifies or even points to the cultic interpretation that Gese presents in his conclusion. In order that readers may see this for themselves, I have

44. 'die als solche, in der Funktion ihrer Verkündigung, ihren Aussagewert haben'.
45. 'Aber auch abgesehen von solchen Differenzen muß grundsätzlich beachtet werden, daß die epische Überlieferung ein spezielles Element des religiösen Lebens darstellt und nicht ein Spiegel der gesamten religiösen Vorstellungswelt sein kann.'
46. 'die einzelnen Erzählungselemente weithin rituellen Charakter haben'.

adduced the six passages in his analysis in which Gese mentions the cult.

(1) KTU 1.1 iv is described as a 'scene of a cultic feast' (1970: 55).[47] Gese does not explain what the cultic element might be. He argues for the cultic character of the scene by referring in a footnote to line 4 of the text: *il.yṯb.b m*[rzḥ...]* (1970: 55 n. 18). The text is reconstructed following KTU 1.114. Even if this reconstruction is correct one would have to note that the *mrzḥ*, as it is presented in KTU 1.1 iv, is more in the nature of a private party. The text is highly fragmented, and the following rendering of its contents is uncertain: At a gathering El asks *ilt* (whoever she might be) and the other gods present to give his son *yw* a new name. The gods urge El to (re)name his son himself. El calls his son *mdd.i[l...]* and warns him against Baal. The scene ends with the slaughtering of oxen, sheep, bulls, rams, calves, lambs and goat-kids. One has to presume that these animals are to be eaten at the banquet. It would hardly be meaningful to claim that the supreme god El is in the process of making sacrifices here—to whom would he be sacrificing? In KTU 1.114 the word *mrzḥ* is also applied to a party, in which no particular cultic element seems present. The word *mrzḥ* seems to have had a twofold meaning: it seems to be the designation of a lodge-like brotherhood, an exclusive club of well-to-do citizens which, under the supervision of a president, holds parties in which intensive wine drinking is a crucial element. *Mrzḥ* may also designate just such a party. The gods were invoked at these parties; but this fact does not make the party or the institution cultic in itself, just as we would not designate a meal in our days as cultic just because it is preceded by a grace. The fact that a religious element (the saying of grace, for instance) is sometimes present during a meal does not make the meal as such a religious phenomenon, nor are all meals cultic in nature. Secondly, in a similar way a *mrzḥ* may be connected with religious elements, but the institution as such is not cultic or religious.

(2) Gese discusses the justification for the seasonal interpretation thus: In an excursus on the combat between Baal and *ym*, Gese contemplates what human experiences might lie at the root of the 'Baal combat-myth' (1970: 59-65). As Gese correctly remarks, the myth contains—although described in the language of myth—natural phenomena such as the changing of the seasons. The myth is, however, more than just an aetiological interpretation of the weather. 'The play

---

47. 'Szene eines kultischen Gelages'.

of forces reveal themselves in the background of the phenomena whose nature extends beyond perceived appearance and belongs to a deeper dimension of experience' (1970: 65).[48] *Ym* and *nhr* symbolize powers of chaos, while the fertilizing rain—and with the rain, thunder—emanates from a heavenly power and recreates the cosmos. Gese also offers an example which suggests that the myth does not follow the changing of the seasons in any very strict way (1970: 68-69), so that his interim conclusion is that:

> The epic thus takes account of the annual seasons when they are required; this, however, is more than a mythical representation of the annual cycle and its rites. Rather, it attempts to adumbrate a history of the god Ba'al and is to be interpreted as a composition on the basis of this goal (1970: 69).[49]

This modification of the importance of the seasonal interpretation forces Gese to dismiss the theories of Gaster in his book *Thespis: Ritual, Myth and Drama*. Gese refrains from giving a ritual interpretation of the Baal-cycle. On the contrary, he puts emphasis on the narrative aspect: the Baal-cycle is the *story* of the god Baal.

(3) KTU 1.3 i contains the 'festal and joyful (sacrificial) meal' of Baal, and it is summarized with the characterization of 'a picture of the joyous Syrian sacrificial cult' (1970: 65).[50] It is questionable whether the scene in question really depicts sacrificial cultic actions. Rather, I think it is an example of the conceptions the people of Ugarit had of a divine (!) banquet.[51] Decisive in this context, however, is the fact that Gese sees the scene as a *representation* of a cultic action; he does not argue that this scene was ever performed in a cultic setting.

48. 'In den Phänomenen offenbart sich hintergründig das Walten von Mächten, deren Wesen über die wahrgenommene Erscheinung hinausgeht und der tieferen Dimension der Wirklichkeit angehört.'

49. 'Das Epos nimmt also jahreszeitliche Bezüge auf, wenn sie sachlich gefordert sind, es ist aber mehr als eine mythische Darstellung des jahreszeitlichen Ablaufs und seiner Riten; es versucht eine Geschichte des Gottes *Ba'al* zu zeichnen und ist kompositorisch von diesem Ziel her zu interpretieren.'

50. 'ein Bild vom freudigen syrischen Opferkult'.

51. Another example of a very human conception of a divine banquet can be found in KTU 1.114. This text, however, is probably not written by Elimilku. It was not found in the library of the high priest. Elements from this text cannot be integrated in the mythological universe of Elimilku.

(4) Gese calls the warlike behaviour of Anat in KTU 1.3 ii a rite of war, a bloody orgy which has 'a sacrifice-like character' (1970: 66).[52] Gese interprets the scene thus: 'The blood that flows in Anat's combat is to be regarded as the newly-released stuff of life which is given the deity' (1970: 67).[53] Gese is, however, speaking about a rite on the level of narrative; he does not say that Anat's bloodshed was actually enacted in the cult! It is true that Baal's invitation to put a 'love- and peace-offering' into the earth (KTU 1.3 iii, lines 15b-17), from the scene which follows immediately after the bloodshed of Anat and the succeeding purification, may reflect a Ugaritic fertility ritual. This hypothesis has been put forward by C. Schaeffer (Schaeffer 1939: 46-47). But this offering, too, takes place on the level of narrative.

(5) Gese believes that Anat's search for Baal in the nether world probably has 'a ritual background'. He refers in this connection to W. Baudissin, *Adonis und Esmun: Eine Untersuchung zur Geschichte des Glaubens an Auferstehungsgötter und an Heilgötter* (Baudissin 1911) and 'die von Frauen durchgeführten Klageriten im Kult der Vegetationsgötter' ('the rites of lament performed by women in the cult of the vegetation gods'; Gese 1970: 72). It is worth noticing that Gese does not say that this scene—Anat's searching for Baal in the nether world—was enacted in the cult; rather, it is the other way round: the scene in question may *reflect* a ritual practice. The narrative is borrowing its imagery from the 'real' world.

(6) According to Gese, it is possible that the wording of 'Anat's attack on Mot' (KTU 1.6 ii, lines 29b-37) may be rooted in a ritual like the one we find in Lev. 2.14 (a cereal-offering of the first fruits of the grain). KTU 1.6 ii, lines 30b-37 runs as follows:

```
30        tiḫd
      bn.ilm.mt.bḫrb
      tbqʿnn.bḫtr.tdry
      nn.bišt.tšrpnn
      brḥm.ttḥnn.bšd
35    tdrʿ.nn.širh.ltikl
      ʿṣr*m*.mnth.ltkly
      npr[m].š*ir.lšir.yṣḥ
```

52. 'einen opferartigen Charakter'.
53. 'Das im Kampf ʿAnats fließende Blut ist wie die freigesetzte Lebenssubstanz anzusehen, die der Gottheit hingegeben wird.'

30   She (*'nt*) seizes the son of the god, *mt*.
        With a sword she splits him,
        with a sieve she spreads him,
        in fire she burns him,
        with a mill-stone she grinds him,
        in the field (35) she scatters him.
        The birds eat his flesh,
        the sparrows devour his limbs.
        Flesh cries out to flesh.[54]

According to Gese, this scene may have had its background in a ritual such as the one we find in Lev 2.14. This text runs:

ואם־תקריב מנחת בכורים ליהוה

אביב קלוי באש גרש כרמל תקריב את מנחת בכוריך

If you present to the Lord a grain-offering of first-fruits of the grain, you must present fresh grain roasted, crushed meal from fully ripened grain (translation from REB).

54. Notes on translation: I have construed *l* in lines 35 and 36 as a particle of confirmation. Another possibility is to translate *l* with 'so that'; thus *TO* I, 260 and Hvidberg-Hansen 1990: I, 115. Cf. Aartun concerning possible translations (Aartun 1974: 34 n. 5).

šir.lšir.yṣḥ (line 37) is indeed enigmatic. Three other possible renderings may be mentioned here: Hvidberg-Hansen (1990: I, 115) divides the Ugaritic text differently and translates:

she sows him on the field,
his flesh, so that the birds may eat,
his limbs, so that the sparr[ows] may devour piece by piece;
he shouts (translation mine).

Margalit suggests that we derive *yṣḥ* from arabic *ṣaḥḥa* (from the root *ṣḥ(ḥ)*), 'heal, return-to-health; become whole again' (1980: 160). In this way Margalit reaches the not very poetic translation: 'Flesh-piece connects to flesh-piece' (1980: 158). 'This rendering will explain the fact that although Anat has resorted to various forms of physical annihilation, Mot, as we learn from col. V, recovers and lives to tell of his discomfiture' (Margalit 1980: 160-61). This rendering is in perfect harmony with one of the main points in the Baal-cycle according to Margalit: namely, 'the indestructibility of Mot, hence the eternity of Death' (1980: 161). It seems, however, as if the translation of the passage in question has been adapted to fit the conclusion.

The authors of *TO* I deny without argument the idea that *yṣḥ* may mean 'shout'. They suggest that the root is the one we also find in the Arabic word *naḍaḥa*, 'sprinkle, splash', and in Hebrew נֵצַח, 'jet of blood', Isa. 63.3, 6 (*TO* I, 260 n. m). On this background *TO* I gives the following conjectural translation (the conjecture is marked by the italic): 'La chair *jaillit* de la chair'.

The wording resembles the Ugaritic text quoted above. The similarity between the two texts has made Gese think that here we have an example of the connection between myth and cult (1970: 73-74).

It is obvious, however, that what makes the first-fruits of the grain in Lev. 2.14 into a sacrifice—that is, an element in a cultic action—is neither the fact that the grain has been roasted nor that the meal has been crushed; rather, it is the fact that the priests sacrifice it according to the laws of sacrifice (compare Lev. 2.15-16 with 2.1-3).

There is nothing to imply a cultic action of this sort in KTU 1.6 ii, lines 30b-37. *'nt* treats *mt* the way a peasant treats the ripe grain. Lines 30b-33 may very well be regarded as the following processes in the course of the harvest: the actual harvesting of the grain, the winnowing (by shovelling the grain, roasting and grinding).[55] The harsh treatment of *mt* has its parallel in the work of peasants, not in the cult.

If one were to adduce an Old Testament parallel to KTU 1.6 ii, lines 30b-37 it would be Exod. 32.20. This text runs:

ויקח את־העגל אשר עשו וישרף באש ויטחן עד אשר־דק
ויזר על־פני המים וישק את־בני ישראל

He took the calf they had made and burnt it; he ground it to powder, sprinkled it on water, and made the Israelites drink it (translation from REB).

In this text three verbs are identical to the Ugaritic text, namely שרף, טחן and זרה (Ugaritic: *šrp*, *ṭḥn* and *dr'*)—even the order is the same. Moses' action in Exod. 32.20 has probably nothing to do with 'Canaanite'[56] fertility cults. The description in Exod. 32.20 underlines Moses' anger and his violent destruction of the golden calf. It is hardly

---

55. Concerning the procedure of harvesting, cf. Dalman 1928, vol. 3. Roasted grain may be grinded to flour, cf. Dalman 1928: III, 263-66. Dalman's *Arbeit und Sitte in Palästina* is an etnographic work which is still highly esteemed (cf. Lemche 1985: 37).

56. The word 'Canaanite' in this book has been placed in inverted commas as a consequence of Lemche 1991. Against the background of an extensive study of extra-biblical and biblical material, Lemche concludes that the 'Canaanites' themselves did not know that they were Canaanites. 'Canaan' and 'Canaanite', in the second and in the first millennium BCE, was always a designation applied *by others* to a not very well defined territory or people in the Syro–Palestinian area. 'Canaan' was divided into a number of city-states ruled by a king and it is not very likely that the inhabitants in one city-state felt politically or ethnically attached to the inhabitants of another city-state. 'Cannanite' is a designation used to describe 'the others'.

meaningful to consider how the cast image of a bull-calf can burn (Exod. 32.4). The effect on the audience is obvious. In addition to this the Israelites are forced to consume a mixture of the powder of the golden calf and water. This final element is part of the destruction of the golden calf and at the same time a punishment for the Israelites. The water is a kind of 'water of cursing' for the Israelites (cf. Num. 5.11-31; Noth 1958: 205).

Gese, however, maintains that KTU 1.6 ii, lines 30b-37 has its background in a rite. Instead of being produced on the altar, the splitted, sieved, burnt and ground-up Mot is spread about on the field. According to Gese, the idea that Mot is spread on the field may be explained as a 'transformation that is essential to the epic narrative' (1970: 73);[57] alternatively, it might have its background in a rite of the cult of Tammuz. In order to substantiate his viewpoint, Gese mentions the mediaeval writer Ibn en-Nedim, who relates that in Harran, in the month of Tammuz, a weeping-ceremony was performed for Tammuz, who had been killed by his master. The bones of Tammuz were crushed between mill-stones and were consequently scattered in the wind. During this ceremonial period the women ate nothing that had been ground in a mill (Gese 1970: 73-74).[58]

But again, Gese does not claim that the scene which he thinks may be derived from cultic rituals has been enacted in cult. I believe that the imagery of the text is derived from the daily life of peasants. The 'scattering' of *mt* is a striking description of complete annihilation; we need not explain that from cultic practices.

Excursus: Tammuz and mt

Gese implicitly raises the question as to whether, in terms of the history of religions, the fertility god Tammuz is related to the Ugaritic god *mt*, 'Death'. This is the topic of this excursus.

In his article 'Toward the Image of Tammuz' (1970) the late Thorkild Jacobsen has presented a very poetic interpretation of the deity Tammuz. If one accepts Jacobsen's interpretation it is clear that the

---

57. 'für die epische Erzählung nötige Abwandlung'.

58. The text of Ibn en-Nedim's book *El-Fihrist* may be found in Chwolsohn 1856: 1-52. Ibn en-Nedim's paragraph on Tammuz can be found in Chwolsohn 1856: 27-28.

concept of Tammuz/Dumuzi[59] in Mesopotamia differs widely from the concept of *mt* in the epic texts from Ugarit.

Tammuz is a Mesopotamian god of vegetation who the ancient Mesopotamians—according to Jacobsen—encountered under four different aspects: (1) as a power in the sap that rises in trees and plants; (2) as a power in the date-palm and its fruits; (3) as a power in grain and beer; and (4) as a power in milk.

Jacobsen thinks to have found a characteristic feature concerning the god Tammuz: 'The power of Tammuz...whether alive or dead, has a character that may be expressed as wholly "intransitive". It does not, either in action or as will and direction, ever transcend the phenomenon in which it dwells' (1970: 75).

Gradually an image of Tammuz presents itself to Jacobsen:

> This aspect of the power in Tammuz as being rather than doing, as having no responsibilities, innocently self-centered, yet pleasing and attractive, is very finely expressed in its symbolization as a young boy, a youth, a symbol shared by all the aspects of Tammuz (1970: 76).

The feelings that people must necessarily have felt towards Tammuz are in perfect harmony with the character of the god: 'The values embodied in the god are such as flow from his role as object of love, youth, and charm, and they blend with qualities of defenselessness and suffering, which invite feelings of pity and compassion allied to those of love' (Jacobsen 1970: 91). The impression one gets of Tammuz from this description differs widely from the impression one gets of *mt* from the Ugaritic texts. Tammuz, for instance, does not take part in conflicts between gods.

> Though Tammuz is a male god, proper manly virtues such as one finds exemplified and celebrated in, for instance, the early epical texts—courage, resourcefulness, steadfastness—are in him almost conspicuously lacking. When he is attacked, or merely fears that he may be attacked, he takes to his heels with no thought of offering resistance (Jacobsen 1970: 91).

---

59. Sumeric *Dumuzi* is often translated as 'the right son'. Jacobsen translates it as 'Quickener of the Child' (Jacobsen 1970: 73); according to Labat the ideogram DUMU means 'son', while ZI basically means 'life' or 'to live' (Labat 1976: 77 and 101).

There is, however, a perhaps less flattering aspect of the deity Tammuz, as Jacobsen presents him: 'In all relationships he seems instinctively to take it for granted that he be only and always receiving' (1970: 91). Jacobsen gives an example of this from Sumerian mythology: Tammuz departs from the realm of death without thinking about his sister, who followed him because of her love for him. Tammuz is apparently willing to leave her to her fate. The boatman speaks on her behalf, and she is rescued and brought into the boat.[60] If one wanted to maintain that Tammuz and Ugaritic *mt* were related in some way one could hypothecate that this negative aspect of Tammuz—the expectation that he should always be on the receiving end—has conceivably developed into the greed that we find in the Ugaritic god *mt*. But that would be pure guesswork, of course.

Weeping was an important element in the cult of Tammuz, as attested in Sumerian texts, in the Gilgamesh-epic, in Ezek. 8.14 and in Ibn en-Nedim. Jacobsen has attempted to describe the emotions that are at the basis of such cultic weeping: 'A close and intimate feeling, then, is the response to the fascinans in Tammuz when not thwarted: a quiet, doting, sensuously contemplative love' (Jacobsen 1970: 99). This emotion, this love for Tammuz, is a necessary condition for the cultic weeping at the death of the deity:

> If thwarted...it becomes a total craving in the soul. And in the cult cycle it is thus thwarted. Having gathered momentum slowly in the happy love which comes to expression in the rite of the wedding, the sacred marriage, it is abruptly and cruelly damned, raised to the point of the unbearable, in the stunned moment of the death of the god. Thus the lament releases it. As it pours forth in full flow in the lament, the intimate closeness of its every image—son, brother, bridegroom—draws directly on depths of real, actual, and immediate emotional experience in the worshipers, encompassing the totality of the emotional relationships in which they stand. Veiled and hidden feeling, longing and sorrows of earlier years, well up in old intensity, all blending with the love for the god, transferring to him, urging toward him to follow him, to die with him:
>
>> If it is demanded, O lad, I will go with you the road of no return...
>> She goes, she goes, to the breast of the nether world.

60. I have not been able to find out what text Jacobsen is referring to here. Jacobsen's article (originally held as a lecture) is lacking in terms of references. It is possibly an as yet unpublished text (cf. Jacobsen 1970: 73, the footnote).

> The daylight fades away, the daylight fades away, to the deepest
> nether world (Jacobsen 1970: 99).[61]

Jacobsen has tried 'to recapture in sympathetic understanding' the emotions of the women taking part in the cult of Tammuz (1970: 73). It is difficult to know if he is right in his description. What is important in our context, however, is that it is virtually impossible to imagine that *mt* would have been met with the same emotions. If one wants to claim that the idea of Tammuz being killed by his lord, crushed between millstones and spread to the winds was also part of the cult of Tammuz in the second millennium BCE (this element in the stories about Tammuz is to my knowledge only present in the writings of the mediaeval writer Ibn en-Nedim and not in the ancient sources), and that this is the rite alluded to in KTU 1.6 ii, lines 29b-37, one has to admit that Elimilku applies the Tammuz-story with much subtlety: The dreadful *mt* receives the same treatment as the beloved Tammuz—and there is no one to bewail him. He even suffers the indignity of being slain by a *female* deity. This goes much beyond the humiliation that Tammuz experiences.

I have scrutinized above (pp. 57-63) the parts of Gese's analysis of the Baal-cycle where he considers the relationship between the cycle and cultic practices. Gese's analysis does not constitute a coherent interpretation of the Baal-cycle as a libretto for a cultic drama. He does not even say that individual passages were enacted in the cult. What he does say is that certain elements of the narrative may have been inspired by a cultic practice.

In Gese's conclusion things are differently weighted. Gese's main point is that the Baal epic tells the story of Baal. That is the result of the analysis of the Baal-cycle and this point is contrasted to the seasonal interpretation. 'The fact that the individual narrative elements are to a large extent of a ritual nature, indeed, that the myth itself may be functionally interpreted, need not contradict this' (1970: 79).[62] With these

---

61. Nils A. Dahl writes: '...Harvard students are reported to have said about... Thorkild Jacobsen: His lectures on Babylonian religion left the impression that he himself believed in Marduk and Ishtar' (Dahl 1988: 11).

62. 'Daß die einzelnen Erzählungselemente weithin rituellen Charakter haben, ja, daß der Mythus funktional interpretiert werden kann, braucht dem nicht zu widersprechen.'

words, Gese introduces an interpretation which has no support in his analysis. As if to reassure the reader, he adds 'Nevertheless, one ought not to go too far in this direction' (1970: 79).[63] But this is precisely what Gese does when, towards the end of his study, he writes:

> It is likely that the Baal epic was not such a free poetic composition that its recital did not have one quite particular '*Sitz im Leben*'. We can only assume that the fixed time of the recital must have been the autumn festival which may have been the New Year festival in both Ugarit and in Israel (1970: 80).[64]

In other words: the necessity of one particular *Sitz im Leben* is postulated and the autumn festival makes its appearance as a *deus ex machina*. And in addition to this, the claim is made that the autumn festival is the only possible *Sitz im Leben*!

Dirk Kinet, 'Theologische Reflexion im ugaritischen Baal-Zyklus'

It is easy—according to Dirk Kinet—to imagine how consciousness of the regular changing of the seasons (or on the mythological level, the certainty of the outcome of the combats between the gods) may have led to a kind of certainty of faith ('Glaubensgewißheit'). During a season of drought it would have been hard to retain this certainty of faith. The function of the Baal-cycle is to be a counterbalance to this presumed popular piety—'Volksfrömmigkeit' (Kinet 1978: 244).

Kinet finds support for his interpretation in two places in particular: KTU 1.4 v 6-9 and KTU 1.4 v 58–vi 15; vii 13-36 ('the window episode').[65]

In KTU 1.4 v 6-9 *aṯrt* says, when El has given his consent to the building of a temple for Baal:

> *wnap.'dn.mṭrh*
> *b*'l.y'dn.'dn.ṯk*t.bglṯ*
> *wtn.qlh.b'rpt*
> *šrh.larṣ.brqm*

63. 'Trotzdem sollte man auch in dieser Hinsicht nicht zu weit gehen.'

64. 'Es ist wahrscheinlich, daß das *Ba'al* epos andererseits noch nicht eine so freie Dichtung war, daß nicht seine Rezitation einen ganz bestimmten "*Sitz im Leben*" hatte. Wir werden als festen Zeitpunkt der Rezitation eigentlich nur das Herbstfest, das in Ugarit wie in Israel Neujahrsfest gewesen sein mag, annehmen können.'

65. The delimitations of paragraphs may be discussed. I do not follow the partitions of Kinet which have no bearing on the interpretation.

And now Baal will fix the time of his rain,
the time of the ships with snow,
his voice in the clouds he will let resound,
the lightnings will light up the earth (Kinet 1978: 242-43).[66]

Kinet presents an example of the idea that Baal sovereignly fixes the time (*'dn...y'dn*) for the coming of the rain: In KTU 1.4 v 58–vi 15; vii 13-36 Baal hesitates to give orders to *ktr.wḫss* about putting a window

---

66. 'Und nun wird Ba'al den Zeitpunkt seines Regens festsetzen, den Zeitpunkt der Schiffe mit Schnee, seine Stimme in den Wolken wird er erschallen lassen, es leuchten auf der Erde die Blitze.' Notes on the translation: I have chosen to present Kinet's translation, even though it is outdated for reasons given below. This translation is, however, necessary if we are to understand Kinet's arguments. Kinet's interpretation is to some extent based on his understanding of the root *'dn*: 'Above all things, the verb or substantive *'dn* is important here. This root expresses more than merely the gift of the rain, as in this text what is important is the fixed point in time at which Ba'al will make his gift of rain. Thus Ba'al's sovereignty in conjunction with this event is emphasized' (1978: 243).

Kinet's interpretation of the mentioned passage presupposes a translation of the Ugaritic root *'dn* as 'fixed time, term' from the Akkadian *adanum*. This Akkadian word has, however, a different root, namely *w'd* (cf. *AHw*, 10). *adanum* is a nominal form of *w'd* (cf. *GAG*, §56r). The corresponding Ugaritic root is *y'd* (cf. *WUS*, no. 1195). It is true there is no attested verb *y'd* in Ugaritic, but three other words *'dt*, *m'd* and *t'dt* may with some certainty be construed as derived from *y'd*. In Hebrew the verb יעד is well known in the sense 'fix'. 'The time that he fixed' is thus: הַמּוֹעֵד אֲשֶׁר יָעֲדוֹ (2 Sam. 20.5).

An even better option is to let the Ugaritic *'dn* equal the Hebrew root *'dn* in the sense 'abundance' and 'exuberance'. In Aramaic *'dn* may mean 'to be' or 'to make abundant', as in, for instance, the tell Fekherye-inscription (published in Abou-Assaf, Bordreuil and Millard 1982; cf. also Greenfield 1984), where the Akkadian *muṭaḫḫidu kibrati* ('which makes the whole world abundant') is translated to Aramaic *m'dn mt kln* ('which makes all the lands abundant'). The well-known Akkadian word *ṭaḫadu* in its G-form means (according to *AHw*, 1378-79), 'to be exuberant' and in the D-form (which is used in the tell Fekherye-inscription) 'to make abundant'. It is therefore reasonable to translate the Aramaic *m'dn* in the tell Fekherye-inscription as 'make abundant'. Greenfield translates against this background KTU 1.4 v 6-9 as: 'And moreover Baal will provide his luxuriant rain, a luxuriant...with overflow; will peal his thunder in the rain clouds, flashing his lightnings to the earth' (1984: 221). Kinet's interpretation is thus weakened for philological reasons. There is, however, reason to discuss it here, since it contains a good attempt at finding a more fruitful understanding of the Baal-cycle than the earlier, more fanciful cultic interpretations. In the main text I will summarize Kinet's interpretation, while accepting for a moment his translation.

in his temple[67]—and thus he also procrastinates with respect to the life-giving rain. In this Baal acts and rules sovereignly—as long as he is capable of doing it.

Kinet interprets what *aṯrt* says here about Baal and the following window episode as a theological attempt at explaining why droughts occasionally occur. It is also a counterbalance to the popular piety mentioned above:

> The advent of Ba'al is certain, but he and he alone determines the time of his arrival. Hence it is not possible for men to force Ba'al to make his gift of the rains. Naturally, this has great consequences for the understanding of sacrifice and cult in Ugarit. And here it must be appropriate again to distinguish between popular piety and the beginnings of theological reflection (1978: 244).[68]

Kinet describes the hypothetical popular piety in the following manner:

> One could easily imagine that the awareness of the ordered course of the seasons, particularly with respect to the once-and-for-all combat among the gods, which can have only one outcome, could soon have led to a simplifying interpretation of reality among the people that was almost governed in detail by rules and qualifications in the manner of a natural law. It was precisely in times of lengthy drought that the certainty of faith in Ba'al's ultimate victory will have been put to a hard test. Here the Ba'al cycle seems to attempt to avoid a conflict between the usual religious conceptions and the realities of the situation of the country (1978: 244).[69]

67. Margalit interprets the window episode quite to the contrary: 'It is our contention that throughout this dialogue, the particle *al* is to be understood as asseverative, and the particle *bl* as the negative. The thrust of this exegesis is to reverse the roles generally ascribed to the actors: It is wise and clairvoyant Kothar who urges "I shan't install windows..." (*bl ašt urbt*); and impetuous Baal who insists "You certainly shall install..." (*al tšt*)' (Margalit 1980: 46). *bl* in a negative sense and *al* with a positive meaning are well testified (cf. *UT*, Glossary nos. 162 and 466, *WUS* nos. 180, 181, 515, 516 and Aartun 1974); as far as I know Margalit is the only one to advocate the interpretation mentioned above.

68. 'Sicher ist Ba'als Kommen, aber er selbst und er allein bestimmen den Zeitpunkt seines Kommens. So kann es nicht in der Macht der Menschen liegen, Ba'al zur Gabe seines Regens zu zwingen. Das hat selbstverständlich große Folgen für das Opfer- und Kultverständnis in Ugarit. Auch hier dürfte wieder zwischen Volksfrömmigkeit und Ansätzen theologischer Reflexion zu unterscheiden sein.'

69. 'Man kann sich ja leicht vorstellen, daß das Bewußtsein um den geordneten

It might be easier to imagine a different reaction during a drought. Rather than assuming that humans have tried to survive the crisis in virtue of their certainty of faith it is more obvious to imagine that the reaction on a period of drought has been a more concrete cultic or at least religious activity—a reaction which, from a modern perspective, would be quite useless.

Kinet's hypothesis about theological reflection in the Baal-cycle is not bad, however, even though we would have to dismiss one of the two examples that he gives. The window episode may be seen as an expression of Baal's hesitation. Through this the sovereignty of Baal is described and thus an explanation of the absence of the rain is given. There is, however, no reason to assume that this theological reflection is intended to be a counterbalance to a popular piety in the way Kinet describes it. Rather, we could expand the theological reflection and make it include the entire Baal-cycle: the sovereign decision of Baal (or perhaps, rather, his fickleness) means that one cannot be sure of the coming of the rain at one particular time. If the seasonal interpretation has something to it (if not in all details then at least insofar as it concerns the basic principles) one might say that not only the weather, but also the changing of the seasons and thus the possibilities for mankind to obtain food are contingent on the internal conflicts of the gods—a fight which man has no influence on, just as little as he can make Baal open the window. The theological message of the Ugaritic Baal-cycle might thus be that the basic conditions of human life are beyond the influence of man.

This is of importance for the understanding of cult in Ugarit. One possibility is what Kinet mentions:

> The episode of the window provides a mythological foundation for Ba'al's interference in natural events; thus a lengthy period without rain finds its explanation in Ba'al's empowerment and sovereignty. The

Ablauf der Jahreszeiten, besonders auch um den ein für allemal sicheren Ausgang der Auseinandersetzungen unter den Göttern, bald zu einer vereinfachenden, einer bis ins Detail naturgesetzlich geregelten und bedingten Wirklichkeitsdeutung unter dem Volk geführt haben kann. Gerade in Zeiten längerer Dürre konnte die Glaubensgewißheit von Ba'als endgültigem Sieg manchmal hart auf die Probe gestellt werden. Der Ba'al-Zyklus scheint hier vermeiden zu wollen, daß die gängigen religiösen Vorstellungen den Realitäten des Landes in allzu krasser Weise widersprechen.'

human prayer for rain, as well as the sacrifices and rites which are performed in this connection, thus provide a further presupposition for the understanding of the Ba'al's power. However, it could not compel Ba'al's interference in natural events (1978: 242).[70]

Another possibility is that when man cannot exercise influence on the gods and the climactic conditions which are of paramount importance for mankind, cultic actions are superfluous.

70. 'Die Fensterepisode [liefert] eine mythologische Begründung für Ba'als Eingreifen in das Naturgeschehen; ein längeres Ausbleiben des Regens findet damit eine Erklärung in Ba'als Eigenmächtigkeit und Souveränität. Das menschliche Bitten um Regen sowie Opfer und Riten, die in diesem Zusammenhang vollzogen werden, schaffen zwar eine weitere Voraussetzung für die Vergegenwärtigung der Herrschermacht Ba'als, erzwingen können sie Ba'als Eingreifen in das Naturgeschehen jedoch nicht.'

Chapter 5

WHERE DID SCHAEFFER FIND THE CLAY TABLETS
OF THE UGARITIC BAAL-CYCLE?*

The above question is a very simple one, and anyone who has ever engaged in Ugaritic studies will know the answer: the clay tablets of the Baal-cycle were found on the acropolis of Ugarit, in the building complex of the high priest. This building complex, as is also well known, was situated between the two great temples of Ugarit. At this point, some scholars have drawn some perhaps over-easy conclusions as to the *Sitz im Leben* of the Baal-cycle. 'This fact [the fact that the library containing the Baal-cycle was situated between the two temples] points already to the probability that the texts found in the library will have to be considered as texts intended for use in the temples, as far as concerns the religious texts at least' (Kapelrud 1952: 17). The question, however, is whether this is sound reasoning, and how we are to understand the term 'religious texts'.

A great variety of texts have been found in the building complex of the high priest of Ugarit: the Baal-cycle, the legends of *krt* and *aqht*, the difficult texts about the Rephaïm, the even more enigmatic text about Shachar and Shalim, ritual texts, letters, lists of deities, etc.[1] Some of these texts are obviously religious texts in the sense that they describe cultic actions; they enumerate the sacrifices, they tell us who is to carry out the sacrifice, how and to which deity. These ritual texts are often extremely difficult to translate partly because of the *termini technici* involved, and partly because they apparently have been written for initiates; the ritual texts were not intended to be introductions to Ugaritic religion for detached spectators. They more likely served as some sort of checklist for the cult personnel who knew the rites already. These

* This chapter was first published as an article in *SJOT* 8.1 (1994), pp. 45-60. Only minor and insignificant changes have been made here.

1.   Some of these lesser-known texts (rituals, correspondence) are given in translation in *TO* II and in *TRU*.

texts are what I shall call 'religious texts', and on this point one must agree with Kapelrud that these ritual texts were presumably 'texts intended for use in the temples'.

The legends of *aqht* and *krt* were found in the archives of the high priest's building complex; these are texts that very few scholars would interpret as cultic texts. They are rather to be described as epic texts. The *Sitz im Leben* is totally unknown. They may have been recited on any big occasion, religious or non-religious; they may have served as school-texts: that is, as texts any well-educated man is supposed to have studied. We do not know. I have chosen the term 'literature' to designate this group of texts.

Somehow between these two groups of texts (the religious texts and the epic literature) is the Baal-cycle. The Baal-cycle is epic in character and has many features in common with *aqht* and *krt*. The main difference is that human beings appear in *aqht* and *krt*, whereas only gods have a role to play in the Baal-cycle—and for this reason the former texts are traditionally called 'legends', the latter 'myths'. However, the Baal-cycle has often been interpreted as a cultic text or even as the 'libretto'[2] of a cult-drama which was performed in one of the temples. This interpretation is, however, dubious.

Another text which is difficult to interpret is KTU 1.23 (SS). Does this text, which apparently contains both epic and ritual elements, belong to the group of rituals, or is it to be construed as part of the epic traditions of Ugarit?

Thus we have a group of texts that are obviously religious texts; we have another group comprising the epic texts *aqht* and *krt*. A third group is correspondence and the like. Some texts are difficult to place in this system of categories—among them SS and the Baal-cycle. SS is difficult to place because it apparently contains both epic and ritual elements. The Baal-cycle has been difficult to place, not because of the text itself (it is obviously an epic text which relates a good story, and for this 'objective' reason the Baal-cycle belongs to the 'literature' of Ugarit together with *aqht* and *krt*), but because of hypotheses made during the history of research. In other words, the question at stake is the *Sitz im Leben* of SS and the Baal-cycle.

Now what has the archaeological find-site to do with the *Sitz im Leben* of, for example, the Baal-cycle? The answer is, not a great deal. It is the texts themselves or, rather, our interpretation of them, that are

2.   Gaster 1950. Cf. pp. 40-52 above.

decisive in this connection. However, when a text does not yield decisive clues to its interpretation it is legitimate to investigate the archaeological context in an attempt to find useful information here (of course
it is always not only legitimate but mandatory to check the archaeological evidence—but in cases where the text is difficult to interpret the
archaeological information might be of greater importance). In the case
of Ugarit it would be interesting to see if there is some kind of pattern
in the way the clay tablets were distributed in the building complex of
the high priest. It would be very useful, indeed, to have correspondence
in one distinctive room or on one 'shelf', ritual texts in another, epics in
another, and so on. This would give us a hint as to how to interpret
some of the more difficult texts: if SS was found in a room that contained exclusively ritual texts, this would be a strong indication that it
should be interpreted as a genuine ritual. If, on the other hand, SS was
found on a 'shelf' or in a room exclusively containing epic literature,
one might for this reason choose to emphasize the epic aspect when
interpreting this text, since the text itself, as mentioned above, does not
yield decisive clues to its interpretation.

   Thus the goal of this investigation is to find out the distribution of
clay tablets in the building complex of the high priest of Ugarit and to
see if from this archaeological material we can add an argument to the
ongoing debate about the *Sitz im Leben* of the Baal-cycle.[3]

   The preliminary excavation reports published in *Syria*, XVI (1935)
give almost no detailed information about the exact find-site of the clay
tablets in question. Two maps[4] (Figures 1 and 2 below) offer some
rough indications as to where in the area of the high priest's building
complex the clay tablets from the first four seasons (1929–32) were
found.

   One might think that it would be fairly easy to indicate the find-site
of the clay tablets and of other objects on a map of the excavated area
(as has actually been done on the map in Figure 1 referred to above)

---

3.   In a popular article Schaeffer even expressed his hope of finding out the
purpose of each room in the building complex of the high priest through a similar
investigation: 'Each slate was carefully measured and photographed for translation,
so that their distribution within the walls might tell us what purpose each room had
served' (*The National Geographic Magazine* 58, 1933: 118).

4.   Figure 1 is reproduced from Claude F.-A. Schaeffer, *Ugaritica III* (MRS, 8;
Paris: Librairie Orientaliste Paul Geuthner, 1956), p. 252 fig. 216; figure 2 is reproduced from *idem, Syria, XVI* (Paris: Librairie Orientaliste Paul Geuthner, 1935),
pl. 36.

and at the same time to publish a list of one's findings, giving each object a locus-number corresponding to the numbers on the map. It was not until 60 years after the discovery of the first text in Ras Shamra, however, that such an enterprise was carried out, as far the epigraphic material is concerned. In 1989, *La trouvaille épigraphique de l'Ougarit*. I. *Concordance* (abbreviated *TEO* I) containing a brief description of all the texts known from Ugarit-Ras Shamra, Minet-el-Beida and Ras ibn Hani with locus-numbers was published. However, there are a few uncertainties, as is also admitted in the preface: '...unfortunately, there remain some difficult cases' (*TEO* I, 5).[5] One of these 'difficult cases' will be studied shortly.

We must concentrate on the first four campaigns (1929–32). This is due to the lack of detailed maps over the excavated areas from the fifth to the eleventh campaign (1933–39). We do, however, possess two good maps, as mentioned above. One of them (Figure 1) is particularly detailed, comprising the 'points topographiques' (abbreviated p.t.) of the first four campaigns (1929–32). And, luckily, it was during these years that the tablets of the Baal-cycle were discovered (and in fact most of the more important texts from the building complex of the high priest).

Practically all the texts that I would describe as religious texts were discovered in a very distinct area (apparently a room) in the western part of the building complex. Most of these texts were found during the first season (1929; cf. the tables at the end of this chapter). The tablets discovered during this season were all found in one particular spot (p.t. 300). On the map in Figure 1 it looks as if this so-called 'nest of tablets' is indicated by a series of small blocks (▮). Right next to this spot is written 'TABLETTES 1929'. The list of deities discovered in 1932 (KTU 1.65) was also found in this area (p.t. 430). However, in 1929 one fragment (KTU 1.13) might be construed as a mythological text. On the other hand it was also possible to interpret the text as some sort of incantation or prayer.[6]

The tablets of the epic texts discovered in 1931 were found in and around a particular room in the southern part of the building complex. No ritual texts were found in this area.

---

5.   '...malheureusement, il subsiste quelques cas difficiles'. Cf. Liverani's critical remarks on the state of publication concerning the royal archives of Ugarit (Liverani 1988).

6.   Cf. the bibliography in *TO* II, 21.

With the exception of KTU 1.7; 1.9; 1.24 and 1.25, which were all
discovered in the 1933 campaign (which means that we have no good
maps to refer their respective *points topographiques* to) and with the
possible exception of the fragmentary texts KTU 1.13 (cf. above) the
rest of the epic texts were discovered during the second campaign, that
is, in 1930. Two of the tablets (KTU 1.14 and 1.17) were found on the
surface—no specific indication of the find-site is given, since surface-
finds can stem from anywhere. Two texts, KTU 1.23 and 4.27, have
been given precise locus numbers. All other tablets—epic as well as
other kinds of texts—from this campaign were, according to *TEO* I,
found at p.t. 210–264—an extremely imprecise piece of information.

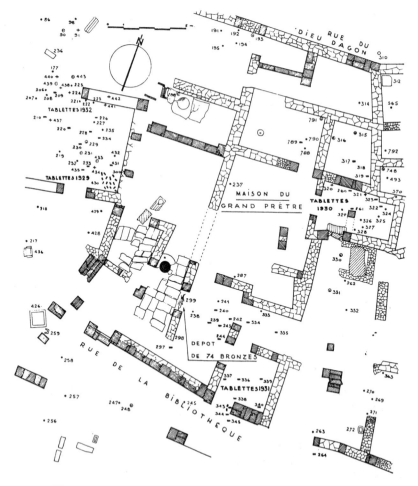

Figure 1. *Map of the building complex of the high priest in Ugarit.*

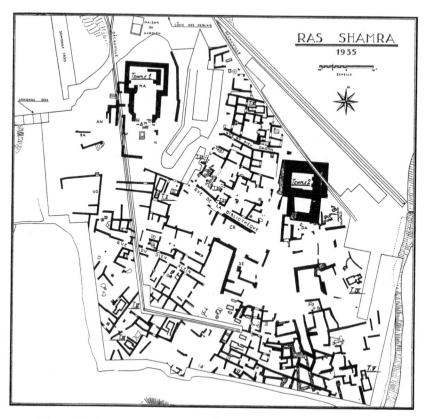

Figure 2. *The excavated constructions at the acropolis of Ras Shamra,*
at the end of the sixth season of excavations (June 1934).

P.t. 210 is situated in the north-western part of the building complex, 264 in the south-east. There is a distance of about 27 m between these two *points topographiques*!

The general indication 'TABLETTES 1930' doesn't help much. 'TABLETTES 1929', 'TABLETTES 1931' and 'TABLETTES 1932' have turned out to be reliable, if rough, indications of where the clay tablets of each season were actually found. On the map 'TABLETTES 1930' is written in a room in the eastern part of the building complex. Yet, on the map in Figure 2 the 'T 30' (which presumably stands for 'TABLETTES 1930'—it doesn't say in the article) is located in another spot—closer to the place where the tablets of the 1931 season were discovered. In any case, the indications 'TABLETTES 1930' and 'T 30' do not correspond very well with the impression that 'p.t. 210–264' yield. According to Schaeffer's own description, the tablets from the second season were found dispersed 'on the entire expanse and even outside the external walls of the monument' (*Syria, XII* [1931]: 81).[7]

The find of a clay tablet is mostly indicated on the map by the sign ▆ (it does not say anywhere that ▆ means clay tablet, but that is the impression one gets) though KTU 2.1 is marked by ☉. One might assume that p.t. 210–264 means that each clay tablet from this season had a locus-number between 210–264 (including 210 and 264)—the exact locus-number of each object no longer being known. If one accepts this assumption it becomes clear that quite a few clay tablets from the second campaign were found in the proximity of the place where the epic texts of the third campaign were discovered. The epic texts discovered in 1930 could come from the whole area of the building complex. However, they may very well all have been found in the proximity of the epic texts from the 1931 season, that is, in the south end of the building complex, for instance at p.t. 239, 240, 242, 243, 244, 248 and 264 (i.e. where 'T 30' is located on the map in Figure 2).[8]

When one thinks about it, it is most likely that clay tablets that contain different parts of the same story, were stored together and therefore have been found close to one another, despite the disorder the destruction of the building may have caused. KTU 1.18 and 1.19 (III D and I D) were both found in 1931 in a distinct area in the southern part of the building complex. It is highly probable that KTU 1.17 (II D) appeared near this place. KTU 1.15 and 1.16 (III K and II K) were discovered in this same area in 1931; presumably, KTU 1.14 (I K) was excavated close to this place. Similarly, it is most likely that, since some parts of the Baal-cycle were found in the southern part of the building complex, the rest of this epic was stored in the same place. But of course we do not know.

In this connection it is interesting to see that KTU 1.23 (SS), which,

---

7.   'Les fouilles de Minet-el-Beida et de Ras Shamra, deuxième campagne (printemps 1930). Rapport sommaire': 'sur toute l'étendue et même en dehors des murs extérieurs du monument'.

8.   One might also suspect that numbers beginning with 2 (201, 202, etc.) stem from the second season, numbers beginning with 3 (301, 302, etc.) from the third and so on. This would make sense in most cases (though not, for instance, the first season). But again it doesn't say anywhere that this is how the recordings have been systematized. Hopefully the editors of *TEO* I or others who are closer to the oral tradition concerning the excavations at Ras Shamra can throw light on this and other questions raised in this chapter.

as pointed out above, apparently contains both epic and ritual elements, was found in the area (perhaps the room?) where the ritual texts were kept.

Conclusions

The goal of this investigation was to discover the distribution of clay tablets in the building complex of the high priest of Ugarit and to see if from this archaeological material an argument could be added to the ongoing debate about the *Sitz im Leben* of the Baal-cycle.

The result of the investigation is that as far as the clay tablets from the campaigns of 1929, 1931 and 1932 are concerned (i.e. tablets about which we possess precise information about the respective find-sites), ritual texts and epic texts were stored separately in the building complex of the high priest in ancient Ugarit. However, in 1930 a number of important epic texts were found, of which we do not know the exact provenance except that they were found in the building complex of the high priest. It is possible and most likely, however, that they were discovered close to the epic texts found in 1931, for the simple reason that all the epic texts from the 1930 season are only parts of greater epics, of which other parts were found in 1931 in one distinct area.

Consequently, Kapelrud's argument mentioned at the beginning of this chapter has to be reversed. The fact that the Baal-cycle was found in the building complex of the high priest does not point to the probability that this text must be considered as a text intended for use in the temples. The fact that the Baal-cycle was (apparently) kept together with the *aqht-* and *krt-*epics (texts that are obviously not cultic texts) and separated from the ritual-texts (among them SS) suggests rather that the Baal-cycle will have to be construed as part of the epic tradition of Ugarit.[9]

9.   Unfortunately, one of the very few investigations of the distribution of texts in ancient archives and libraries, Olof Pedersén's *Archives and Libraries in the City of Assur*, does not help here in terms of terminology. Pedersén distinguishes between libraries and archives: 'Each group of interrelated texts is here classified either as a library or an archive. "Library" describes a group of literary texts in the widest sense of the the word, including for example lexical texts. "Archive" describes a group of texts of administrative, economic, juridical and similar types, including letters' (Pedersén 1985: 20-21). However, this neat distinction is not watertight, of course: 'The occurrence of a few texts of the opposite type has not led to a classification change from library to archive or vice versa, but when there

But of course this argument has to be applied carefully. It is only one argument—and indeed a minor one—in a more comprehensive interpretation of the Baal-cycle.

The Sitz im Leben *of the Baal-cycle*

Well then, one asks, what is the *Sitz im Leben* of the Baal-cycle? We shall probably never know for sure. In the history of research a cultic role has been presumed, but a good reason why the epic in question has to be construed as a cultic text has never been given. The cultic *Sitz im Leben* has simply been taken for granted.

As mentioned above, we do not know the *Sitz im Leben* of the Baal-cycle. The epic relates a magnificent story about gods. And this story makes sense in itself as a story (apart from obscure passages, unknown words and lacunae which always appear in literature of this age). For this reason the cultic interpretation is superfluous. Cultic texts are among other things characterized by the fact that they need to be completed by actions in order to be fully understandable.[10]

Perhaps the Baal-cycle was recited in the court of the king. Maybe the epic was recited at a festival, just as *Enuma Elish* was recited during

are any considerable number of texts of the opposite categories, the collection is described as a library with archive' (Pedersén 1985: 21). Thus, it is not surprising when Pedersén writes in his conclusion: 'According to the definitions used here, literary texts, in the broad sense of the word, are found in libraries, and documents, in the the broad sense of the word, in the archives. The libraries are often combined with archives' (Pedersén 1986: 145). It appears that the terminological distinction library/archive is not parallelled in the Mesopotamian material that Pedersén uses. Compare, for instance, the Neo-Assyrian library with archive in the Aššur temple, a library/archive which contained a vast variety of material: King inscriptions, royal decrees, texts concerning deliveries to the temple, lists of persons, lexical lists, regulations concerning palace and harem life, a tablet with laws, cultic texts, royal rituals, etc. (description by Pedersén 1986: 12-28). Now, which of these texts makes the library a library *with archive*? This question may not have been meaningful to the organizer of the library/archive in question.

10. In fact the Baal-text does not correspond very well to, for instance, Mowinckel's description of the cultic words: 'Jedoch gerade weil Wort und Handlung zusammengehören, bleibt der Text oft nur bruchstückhaft; er muß überall durch die Handlungen ergänzt werden, um völlig verständlich zu werden. Deshalb bieten die alten kultdramatischen Texte sehr oft einen so unvollständigen und unzusammenhängenden Eindruck; von den Handlungen, die sie einmal ergänzt haben, wissen wir meist wenig' (Mowinckel 1953b: 112).

the *Akītu* festival.[11] Maybe it was a school-text—part of the literature that every educated man should know.

Or perhaps the priests of Ugarit had appropriated[12] the Baal-cycle for the reason that it contains an anticultic potential. The Baal-cycle is the story about Baal and his conflicts with *ym* and *mt*. The results of these struggles are of decisive importance for man (causing rain and drought), but man cannot intervene in them. Thus the epic tells us that certain (climatic) conditions—that are vital to the human race—lie beyond the influence of man. And for this reason cultic exertions are superfluous. This is the anticultic potential of the Baal-cycle.

One might object that the last view presented here is a very Protestant one. And perhaps it is. But it is just as 'possible' as a cultic interpretation, and the only reason for presenting it here is to show the diversity of possible interpretations of the Ugaritic Baal-cycle.

Alphabetical Cuneiform Tablets Found at Ras Shamra-Ugarit during the First Four Seasons (1929–32)
The following list contains only alphabetical texts published in *CTA* or *KTU* (or both). *TEO* I enumerates a few less important texts that have not been published in *CTA* or *KTU*. Moreover, a number of fragments from the first 11 campaigns are known 'to which it has proved impossible to attribute a precise year and provenance' (*TEO* I, 64; cf. *TEO* I, 64-73).

I have described the well-known mythological texts KTU 1.1–1.25 only through Virolleaud's abbreviations.

11. Cf. the ritual text of the *Akītu* festival in *ANET*, 331-34. Note, however, that this recital takes place without any kind of enactment. It is said that during the recital the priests perform 'their rites in the traditional manner'—an otherwise often employed turn of speech when apparently well-known rites are to be performed (cf. lines 38, 185 [reconstruction], 277 and 336).

12. I have borrowed the idea of appropriation from Tilde Binger's prize essay delivered to the University of Copenhagen in January 1992. I myself originally explained the anticultic potential of the Baal-cycle by suggesting that its *Sitz im Leben* might have been recitation at the royal court, and that the ideology of the court was not necessarily identical with that of the priests of Ugarit. The reason that this anticultic text was found in the precinct of the high priest could be that the scribal school was situated here. It was the job of the scribes to produce texts for recitation at the court, whether or not the high priest approved of the content of the epics. The idea of appropriation, however, makes the anticultic potential of the Baal-cycle easier to explain.

I am very much dependent for the description of contents on work presented in *CTA*, *UT* and *TO* II. By means of this list I intend merely to give a survey of the texts in question and not new independent interpretations.

A number of syllabic texts were also discovered on the premises of the high priest. However, these texts are all lexical or gramatical texts or letters and are consequently not of importance in this connection. One syllabic text (Ugaritica V, nos. 128-129) might be construed as a list of deities. It was discovered in 1929 in the 'nest of tablets' at p.t. 300.

Alphabetical Cuneiform Tablets from the 1929 Season

CTA	KTU	Points Topo-graphiques	Contents
13	1.13	300	Fragmentary
27	1.45	300	Fragmentary
29	1.47	300	List of deities
31	4.15	300	List
32	1.40	300	Ritual texts
33	1.43	300	Ritual texts
34	1.39	300	List of sacrificial animals
35	1.41	300	List of sacrificial animals
36	1.46 + 7.41	300	Ritual texts
37	1.49	300	Fragmentary. List of sacrifices
38	1.50	300	Fragmentary. List of sacrifices
39	1.48	300	Fragmentary. List of sacrifices
40	1.27	300	Fragmentary. List of sacrifices?
43	1.58	300	Fragmentary
44	1.56	300	Fragmentary
45	1.57	300	Fragmentary
47	1.53	300	Fragmentary
54	2.3	300	Fragmentary. Letter
55	2.4	300	Letter
56	2.6	300	Fragmentary. Letter
58	2.5	300	Fragmentary. Letter
60	2.8	300	Fragmentary. Letter?
62	2.7	300	Fragmentary. Letter
63	7.29 + 7.30	300	Fragmentary. Letter?
98	4.13	300	List
101	4.12	300	List of names
107	4.16	300	List of names
108	4.21	300	Fragmentary. List of names

CTA	KTU	Points Topo-graphiques	Contents
112	5.1	300	Writing exercise? List of names
130	4.19	300	Fragmentary
138	4.22	300	Fragmentary
142	4.14	300	List of goods
150	4.20	300	Fragmentary
151	4.18	300	Fragmentary
155	4.10	300	Fragmentary
166	1.42	300	Hurrian Texts. Religious contents
168	1.44	300	Hurrian Texts. Religious contents
169	1.54	300	Hurrian Texts. Religious contents
170	1.52	300	Hurrian Texts. Religious contents
171	1.32 + 1.33	300	Hurrian Texts. Religious contents
174	1.34	300	Hurrian Texts. Religious contents
175	7.43	300	Hurrian Texts. Religious contents
176	1.59	300	Hurrian Texts. Religious contents
177	1.35 + 1.36	300	Hurrian Texts. Religious contents
180	1.51	300	Hurrian Texts. Religious contents
182	7.24	300	Hurrian Texts. Religious contents
183	7.42	300	Hurrian Texts. Religious contents
185	7.25	300	Hurrian Texts. Religious contents
194	7.27	300	Fragmentary
195	7.46	300	Fragmentary
196	1.55	300	Fragmentary
199	4.17	300	Fragmentary
200	4.17	300	Fragmentary
201	7.33	300	Fragmentary
203	7.34	300	Fragmentary
204	7.35 + 7.36	300	Fragmentary
205	7.37	300	Fragmentary
211	7.44	300	Fragmentary
212	7.45	300	Fragmentary
214	7.38	300	Fragmentary
216	7.39	300	Fragmentary
217	7.40	300	Fragmentary
–	4.13	300	List
–	4.5	300	Fragmentary. List
–	1.37	300	Fragmentary

Alphabetical Cuneiform Tablets from the 1930 Season

CTA	KTU	Points Topo-graphiques	Contents
3	1.3	210-64	V AB
4	1.4	210-64	II AB
5	1.5	210-64	I* AB
6	1.6	210-64	I AB
12	1.12	210-64	BH
14	1.14	surface	I K
17	1.17	surface	II D
21	1.21	210-64	II Rp
22	1.22	210-64	III Rp
23	1.23	209	SS
26	1.62	210-64	Fragmentary. Myth?
61	2.9	210-64	Fragmentary. Letter
68	4.27	201	List. Cities?
100	4.25	210-64	Fragmentary. List
110	4.26	?	Fragmentary
172	1.60	210-64	Hurrian list of deities
140	4.4	210-64	List
148	4.23	210-64	Fragmentary
197	1.61	210-64	Fragmentary
198	7.31	210-64	Fragmentary
–	7.48	210-64	Fragmentary
–	7.49	210-64	Fragmentary

Alphabetical Cuneiform Tablets from the 1931 Season

CTA	KTU	Points Topo-graphiques	Contents
1	1.1	345	VI AB
2	1.2	338, 343, 341	III AB
8	1.8	339	II AB var.
10	1.10	337	IV AB
11	1.11	338	IV AB III*
15	1.15	338, 343, 341	III K
16	1.16	335	II K
18	1.18	338, 343, 341	III D
19	1.19	343	I D
20	1.20	338, 343, 341	I Rp
28	1.63	334	Fragmentary
57	2.1	331	Letter
59	2.2	296	Letter?

CTA	KTU	Points Topo- graphiques	Contents
77	4.29	340	List
149	4.30	304	Fragmentary. List
167	1.64	344	Hurrian text

Alphabetical Cuneiform Tablets from the 1932 Season

CTA	KTU	Points Topo- graphiques	Contents
30	1.65	430	List of deities
53	2.10	431	Letter

Chapter 6

ENUMA ELISH AND THE AKĪTU FESTIVAL

When scholars have tried to identify the *Sitz im Leben* of the Baal-cycle they have often used the so-called Babylonian 'epic of creation' *Enuma Elish* as a parallel. This chapter is dedicated to determining what we can possibly know about the *Sitz im Leben* of *Enuma Elish*.

As far as I have been able to find out, only two Akkadian texts explicitly refer to the use of *Enuma Elish*: namely, the ritual-text of the New Year festival in Babylon[1] and VAT 9555 (duplicate: VAT 9538).[2]

The Ritual-Text of the Akītu Festival

In the first of these texts, the ritual-text of the Babylonian *Akītu* festival, we are told that *Enuma Elish* is to be recited in front of the god Bel on the fourth day of the month of Nisan. A great many ritual acts are described in the rest of the ritual-text (which is why it is called a ritual-text!); the recitation of *Enuma Elish*, however, stands isolated from these actions: After a description of the rites that various cult-servants perform on the fourth day of the month of Nisan 'according to tradition' (GIN$_7$ *šá* DIŠ-*a = kîma ša ginâ*), the text runs:

> [*e-nu-m*]*a an-na-a i-te-ep-šú*
> 280 [*arki tar*]-*din-nu šá ki-iṣ u$_4$-mu e-nu-ma e-liš*
> [*ištu ri-š*]*i-šú* EN TIL-*šú* ^{lú}ŠEŠ.GAL *é.umuš.a*

---

1. 'Le rituel des fêtes du nouvel an à Babylone', in Thureau-Dangin 1921: 127-54. The text has been transmitted in four fragments: DT 15, DT 114, DT 109 and MNB 1848. The tablets probably date from the Seleucid period; they are presumably copies of tablets which are now lost. Translations of the text—apart from the one in Thureau-Dangin 1921—can be found in *ANET*, 331-34 (translation by A. Sachs) and in *ANET*'s predecessor, *AOT*, 295-303 (translation by E. Ebeling).

2. Concerning the reconstruction of the text, cf. von Soden 1955: 132-33.

[*ana* ^dEN *i*]-*na-áš-ši ma-la šá* U₄ *e-liš*
ana ^dEN [*i*]-*na-áš-šu-u* IGI *šá* AGA *šá* ^dGÍŠ
u KI.DÚR *šá* ^d*En-líl ku-ut-tu-mu-u*

[Whe]n they have done this
280   the *šešgallu*(-priest) from the House of Command[3]—[after the cu]lt
      meal at the end of the day—shall recite *Enuma eliš* [from the begin]-
      ning to the end
      [in front of Bel]. While he recites *Enuma eliš*
      in front of Bel, the front of the tiara of Anu
      and the seat of Enlil shall be covered.

In other words, there is no evidence in this text that a cultic drama took place in connection with the recitation. It is not even said that during the recitation the priests performed 'their rites according to tradition' (ME-*šú-nu* GIN₇ *šá* DIŠ-*a*—or in transcription: *parṣêšunu kîma ša ginâ*), an otherwise frequently used turn of speech when apparently well-known rites are to be performed (as, for example, in lines 38, 185 [reconstructed], 277 and 336). The separation of the recitation and the cultic actions of that day is marked by a dividing line in the text between lines 278 and 279. The verb *inašši* probably does not mean anything other than 'recite', or perhaps 'recite with a lifted hand'.[4]

Svend Aage Pallis, in his conprehensive study on the Babylonian New Year festival, does not construe *Enuma Elish* as a cult-text. Pallis prefers to call the epic a 'cult legend' (1926: 267): that is, 'originally a cult-text which has developed independently and in part become distinct from the cult' (1926: 250). This view tallies with the considerations presented in a more recent study:

> A cult-drama in the sense of a dramatic enactment of *Enuma eliš* has surely not taken place. On the other hand, text-genres such as cult-commentaries make clear, that ritual acts may symbolize mythical events or may be subject to mythical interpretations (Pongratz-Leisten 1994: 74).[5]

---

3.   *é.umuš.a* = House of Command, a designation for the cella of the Marduk-temple Esangila in Babylon (cf. George 1993: 156).
4.   *našum* generally means 'to lift, carry'. *CAD* notes only two instances where the verb carries the meaning 'to recite' (*CAD* s.v., paragraph 1j). Von Soden translates *inašši* in this connection as 'vortragen' (cf. *AHw*, 764). Thureau-Dangin translates it as 'élèvera' and explaines in a footnote, 'C'est-à-dire "récitera la main levée"' (Thureau-Dangin 1921: 136). Sachs mentions Thureau-Dangin's suggestion, 'the *urigallu*-priest...shall recite (while lifting his hand?)' (*ANET*, 332).
5.   'Ein Kultdrama im Sinne einer dramatischen Aufführung von *Enuma eliš* hat sicherlich nicht stattgefunden. Andererseits lassen Textgattungen wie die

This leads us to the cult-commentary VAT 9555.

VAT 9555/9538

To my knowledge the only other text which explicitly mentions what *Enuma Elish* was used for is VAT 9555/9538.[6] The epic is mentioned twice; both cases have to do with recitation.

When one reads the two textual witnesses in combination, the lines in which *Enuma Elish* is mentioned run as follows:

34 *e-nu-ma e-liš ša da-bi-ib-u-ni ina* IGI ᵈEN *ina* ᴵᵀᵁBÁR *i-za-mur-ú-šú-ni ina* UGU *ša ṣa-bit-u-ni*

54 *šu-ú ina* ŠÀ *e-nu-ma e-liš iq[-ta/qi-bi] ki-i* AN-*e* KI-*tim la ib-ba-nu-ni* AN.ŠÁR *it-[tab-ši]*
ki-i URU *u* É *ib-šu-u-ni šu-ú it-tab-ši*

34 *Enuma Elish*, which they recite in front of Bel (and which) they sing in Nisan, is about the one they have taken prisoner.

54 It is said in *Enuma Elish*: When Heaven and Earth were not created, Aššur came i[nto being].
(Only) when city and temple (already) existed, did he come into being.[7]

These two lines do not refer to any kind of enactment of *Enuma Elish*. In terms of 'what the poem was used for' they mention nothing but recitation. Lines 54-55 contain a reference of *Enuma Elish* according to the Assyrian version.

Of course, rituals *did* take place in Assyrian and Babylonian religion, but the close connection between mythical texts (*in casu Enuma Elish*) and rituals is not obvious. Alasdair Livingstone concludes:

Kultkommentare erkennen, daß rituelle Handlungen mytische Ereignisse symbolisieren oder eine mythische Ausdeutung erfahren können...'

6. Concerning the interpretation of this highly difficult text, cf. my review of Theodor Herzl Gaster's *Thespis: Ritual, Myth and Drama* in Chapter 4 of this book (pp. 40-52) and Livingstone 1989.

7. Cf. Livingstone 1989: 85. Notes on transliteration and translation: line 34: *i-za-mur-ú-šú-ni*: As von Soden has rightly pointed out, *ú* is missing in VAT 9538 (von Soden 1955: 136 n. 2; line 34 in VAT 9538 can be found in KAR no. 219 obv line 8). In Neo-Assyrian the cuneiform character for *mur* can, however, carry the phonetic value *muru* (cf. Labat 1976, sign no. 401: 187). It is thus not necessary to transliterate *i-za-mur-šú-ni*, as Frymer-Kensky does (Frymer-Kensky 1983: 134). *izammurušuni* probably reflects the right understanding, as it is a possible transcription of both textual witnesses. The two texts conform with each other in all essentials.

In a cult drama one would expect a myth to be developed from episode to episode through the various stages of a ritual. But this is not the case in the explanatory works. Individual actions in, or details of, a ritual are each equated with what can only be regarded as a whole myth. To suppose that the ritual enacted myth one would have to imagine that whole myths were repeatedly acted in widely differing minute actions of the ritual. One would also have to imagine that the same myth was enacted in different ways in the same ritual. These considerations show that religious or cult drama in the sense of a conscious enactment of myth is not involved (Livingstone 1986: 167).

Conclusion

Against the background of the Babylonian ritual-texts there is no basis for hypothecating that *Enuma Elish* was used as a kind of libretto, or that it was accompanied by cultic actions at all. The recitation of the epic during the *Akītu* festival was an event in its own right. As I have pointed out above, the priests do not even perform 'their rites according to tradition', *parṣêšunu kîma ša ginâ*, an otherwise frequently employed turn of phrase when formerly well-known, but now unknown, rites are to be performed.

In the epilogue of *Enuma Elish* we have a clear hint as to the use—that is, the *Sitz im Leben*—of the poem. Again, no enactment is mentioned.

> With the title 'Fifty' the great gods
> Proclaimed him whose names are fifty and made his way supreme.
> Let them be kept (in mind) and let the leader explain them.
> Let the wise and the knowing discuss (them) together.
> Let the father recite (them) and impart (them) to his son.
> Let the ears of shepherd and herdsman be opened.
> Let him rejoice in Marduk, the Enlil of the gods,
> 150 That his land may be fertile and that he may prosper.
> Firm in his order, his command unalterable,
> The utterance of his mouth no god shall change.
> When he looks he does not turn away his neck;
> When he is angry, no god can withstand his wrath.
> Vast is his mind, broad his sympathy,
> Sinner and transgressor may come before him.
> ...
> He wrote down and (thereby) preserved (it) for the future.
> The [*dwell*]ing of Marduk which the gods, the Igigi, had made,

160   ...let them speak.
    ...the song of Marduk,
    [Who] vanquished Ti[amat] and achieved the kingship.[8]

The 50 honorary names of Marduk which are enumerated on tablet VI, line 121–tablet VII, line 136, are, strictly speaking, what the epilogue is about; they can, however, be construed as *pars pro toto*: it is the poem in its entirety which is to be 'kept in mind, explained, discussed, recited', etc.

It is possible, of course, that the Baal-cycle was recited during a cultic festival of some kind in the same way as *Enuma Elish*. But even if one should conjecture that that was the case (and there is nothing in the Ugaritic material which suggests it was) the idea of a *dramatic enactment* of the poem is merely free fantasy. Indeed, not even in the Babylonian material concerning *Enuma Elish* do we have the slightest hint of enactment of any kind—quite the contrary.

Considering how little we can actually know about the *Sitz im Leben* of the Baal-cycle, the hypothesis concerning the enthronement festival of Baal must be said to be groundless guesswork. What is important in this connection is that there is no testimony referring to any kind of enthronement festival in the Ugaritic ritual texts (Cf. *TO* II, *TRU* and Tarragon 1980).

The study of the Ugaritic ritual texts is extremely difficult. That is a fact known by anyone who has ever tried to tackle these often fragmentary and often almost incomprehensible texts.

It is very illustrative that volume 2 of Paolo Xella's *I Testi Rituali di Ugarit* has not yet been published (volume 1 came out in 1981). The second volume—'in an advanced phase of the editing procedure'—is to contain

> a series of specific historical-religious and philological researches of the materials examined which run from themes of fundamental importance (the typology of ritual; the materials of sacrifice; the class and morphology of the various deities, and the like) to more limited problems (as, for example, the study of the cult on the basis of the myths and the economic texts; the role of the king in the sacrifice; the Ugaritic calendar; the analysis of specific features of the cult, and the like) (*TRU*, 17).[9]

    8.   Quoted from Speiser's and Grayson's translation in *ANET*, 72 and 503.
    9.   'una serie di specifiche recerche storico-religiose e filologiche sui materiale esaminati, che vanno da temi di importanza fondamentale (le tipologie rituali; la

It is interesting that Mowinckel did not think that the ritual- and sacrificial laws of the *Priesterschrift* (the priestly document) could be used as a point of departure for a description of Israelite cult.[10] Right or wrong though he may be on this point, the ritual texts from Ras Shamra must be evaluated differently: they must form the basis for any description of the Ugaritic cult.

Now de Langhe was also a good minimalist concerning the *Sitz im Leben* of the Baal-cycle. His conclusion runs:

> The existence of these 'dramatic performances' needs to be proved, other than by the presence of the cycle in question. It is no doubt true that no one would think of calling in question the existence of the temple of Baal, the custom of offering him sacrifices, the outstanding place of the god Baal in the pantheon of Ugarit, and his decisive role in maintaining and renewing the fertility and well-being of persons and things. One might even admit *a priori* the possibility of 'dramatic performances' at regular intervals. But the question still remains: what role did the cycle of texts AB play in it? The only answer yielded by the examination and analysis of the texts under discussion is a myth with epic aspects. All the rest dissolves into hypothesis (de Langhe 1958: 141).

To sum up: Mowinckel's theories about an enthronement festival of Yahweh are not in any way supported by the Ugaritic material. *There is no evidence that an enthronement festival was ever celebrated in Ugarit.*

materia sacrificale; ruolo e morfologie delle varie divinità ecc.), a problemi più circoscritti (come ad esempio l'esame dei dati sul culto desumibili dai miti e dai testi economici; il ruolo del re nei sacrifici; il calendario ugaritico; l'analisi di tratti specifice del culto, ecc.)'.

10. '...The legal contents of the *Priesterschrift* represents a very casual selection made according to certain one-sided criteria...The impression one receives of Israel's cult is that it was mainly a dull sacrificial cult and that the most important thing next to the sacrifice was the fees to the priests and the levites. This is highly one-sided, if not false, and it does not even apply to the time of Judaism that the book dates from' (Mowinckel 1924a: 14; my translation). 'It is...clear how little the *Priesterschrift* has to do with real cult-religion, and that even Deuteronomy with its programme of cult-reform is really a testimony of the incipient sclerosis of the Israelite cult-religion' (Mowinckel 1924a: 16; my translation).

Chapter 7

CONCLUSIONS

In the history of research, much emphasis has been put on possible connections and differences between Ugaritic and Israelite religion. This book is centred on one aspect in that connection. Scholars have been prone to construe the Ugaritic Baal-cycle as a cult-text accompanying the enthronement of Baal. After the conquest of Canaan, the Israelites are supposed to have adopted this festival from the Canaanites and transferred it to the worship of Yahweh. Thus scholars think they have confirmed Mowinckel's theory about the enthronement festival of Yahweh, a thesis which was proposed before the discovery of the Ugaritic texts. In the preceding chapters I have dismissed this construction. There is no evidence that an enthronement festival was ever celebrated in Ugarit.

Ugaritic religion has been regarded as synonymous with Canaanite religion. The difference between Ugaritic or Canaanite religion on the one hand and Yahwism on the other has been much emphasized by scholars who have taken over in an uncritical way the abhorrence of the Old Testament prophets towards 'Canaanite' religion. Albright's view on the development of the religion is clearly expressed in the title of his book: *Yahweh and the Gods of Canaan: A Historical Analysis of Two Contrasting Faiths* (1968). Notice also Albright's remark on 'the extremely low level of Canaanite religion, which inherited a relatively very primitive mythology and had adopted some of the most demoralizing cultic practices then existing in the Near East... The brutality of Canaanite mythology... passes belief..' (1961: 338)[1] Oldenburg also succeeds in entering into the spirit of the biblical prophets concerning the abhorrence of Canaanite religion: 'The more I studied pre-Israelite religion, the more I was amazed with its utter depravity and wicked-

1. This is also quoted by Lemche as an example of Albright's and his disciples' lacking understanding of 'Canaanite' religion (Lemche 1985: 60-61 n. 92).

ness. Indeed there was *nothing* in it to inspire the sublime faith of Yahweh. His coming is like the rising sun dispelling the darkness of Canaanite superstition' (1969: xi). 'How could anything good come out of Canaan?' (1969: 172). 'In sharp contrast to the character of both El and Yahweh the rest of the gods of Canaan were amoral nature gods. None was like El and Yahweh' (1969: 173). I believe that this attitude does not further an adequate understanding of the material. Liverani, on the other hand, has presented some very sensible considerations on the interest of some scholars in furthering a particular (biblical) understanding of the history of Israel and the problems their attitude entails (Liverani 1980).

In comparing the theories about the enthronement festivals of Baal and Yahweh, I have studied the Ugaritic and Old Testament materials separately. This procedure is necessary if one wants to avoid rash conclusions. The result is, however, that there is no real basis for a comparison left—at least concerning a possible enthronement festival.

A description of Ugaritic religion should have the ritual texts as its point of departure. The *Sitz im Leben* of the Baal-cycle is a question not yet answered.

The Anticultic Potential of the Baal-cycle

In the preceding chapters I have shown that the theory about the Ugaritic Baal-cycle being a cultic text is untenable. The Baal-cycle is a single, coherent story which makes sense outside a cultic context. Thus the Baal text is different from cultic texts (the texts which accompany a cultic drama) which—at least according to Mowinckel—have to be 'complemented with actions in order to be fully understandable' (Mowinckel 1950: 98; my translation).

On the other hand, it is clear that this does not exclude the possibility that the Baal-cycle may have been recited at a religious festival, just as *Enuma Elish* was recited at the Babylonian *Akītu* festival (cf. Chapter 6); there is, however, nothing to imply that this was the case. The Baal-cycle may have been recited in one of the temples on an annual day of celebration, or at the royal court, at parties of a more private character, or even in the meetings of a sectarian movement (the text might in that case have been appropriated by the Ugaritic priests), or the text may have been used in connection with the education of young men. Perhaps it was considered *the* classical text that every man should know. The possibilities are legion.

The viewpoint that the Baal-cycle is not a cultic text has now and
again been advanced in the history of research. Margalit, for instance,
suggests a 'literary approach' to the Baal-cycle, 'one which has as its
first postulate the recognition of the text as quintessentially and above
all else a story!' (Margalit 1980: 205). But even Margalit sees a cultic
enactment—if not as necessary, then at least as plausible—as: 'Less
easily demonstrated, but nevertheless highly probable, is the hypothesis
of a ritual enactment of at least certain portions of the story, this re-
enactment reflected occasionally in the literary fabric as well (literary
reflex of ritual being the alternate aspect of myth/literature realized as
ritual)' (Margalit 1980: 204). There is nothing to support this conclusion in Margalit's analysis of the Baal-cycle. Margalit is simply stuck
in the traditional view that myth is a projection of cultic acts.[2] M.S.
Smith also mentions the possibility that the Baal-cycle is not a cultic
text: 'The Baal-cycle may not be a liturgical text at all, but one which
draws on the imagery of the autumn...' (M.S. Smith 1986: 331-32).
Smith, however, does not expand on this view.

It is fascinating, however, that when one has realized that the *Sitz im
Leben* of the Baal-cycle is not necessarily religious or cultic in character it then becomes clear that the cycle may give rise to a number of different (and perhaps even mutually exclusive) interpretations, as all
good stories do. I shall myself present a new interpretation below. I
cannot prove that it is 'correct' and I will not insist that this was how
the ancient citizens of Ugarit understood the epic. However, I am prepared to claim that the interpretation presented is just as adequate as a
cultic interpretation, though it may not be as impressive. Impressive
hypotheses (such as Mowinckel's or Gaster's) are, however, not necessarily true.

The Baal-cycle is the story about Baal and his conflicts with *ym* and
mt. The outcome of these fights are of decisive importance for man
(causing rain and drought), but man cannot intervene in the fray. Thus
the epic tells us that certain (climatic) conditions—which are vital to
the human race—lie beyond the influence of man. And for this reason
cultic exertions are superfluous. This is the anticultic potential of the
Baal-cycle.

If this interpretation is adequate, theological reflection on the Baal-

2.   A devastating critical analysis of Margalit's method may be found in Renfroe 1986: 56-74.

cycle is not limited to single paragraphs, such as Kinet presumes.[3] On the contrary, the anticultic element permeates the entire narrative. One might feel tempted to say that the Baal-cycle contains an anticultic ideology or theology.

By the word 'ideology', I understand a body of ideas that a person, group of persons or an entire society acts according to (or they think they act according to; it may actually be the case that they are acting, whether consciously or unconsciously, against it). The word 'theology' may be used in more or less the same way, but in a more specific area. If one wants to claim that the Baal-cycle was written consciously as a counterbalance to the temple cult, one could speak of an anticultic ideology. One could also imagine, however, that the Baal-cycle replenished an ideological vacuum at a time when religious exertions were minimal, and hence that the anticultic element in the narrative is not an example of a conscious ideology. Perhaps neither Elimilku nor his (presumed) audience knew that the Baal-cycle possessed an anticultic potential. This particular story became popular, however, because it answered the need for an interpretation of reality, whether this need was expressed explicitly or not.

Consciousness is characterized by the explicit expression of what one is conscious about. In narratives, the attitudes or ideology of the author are not necessarily expressed explicitly, and one might therefore wonder whether the author of a fictional work is actually conscious about the 'ideology' that one might uncover through a literary analysis.

Thus one might wonder to what degree the Danish author Karen Blixen was conscious of the theology contained in her narratives, if it were not for the fact that we find explicit reflections about Christianity in her letters that correspond to the views implicitly presented in the stories (cf. Bjerg 1989: 11-12).

Another example of a literature which has become world famous without its author or its readers being conscious about what is going on in the stories is provided by the fairy tales of Hans Christian Andersen. It is reasonable to assume that neither the author nor most of his readers have achieved such a consciousness about the author's fairy tales as the one presented in the psychological study of Eigil Nyborg, *The Inner Outline of the Fairy Tales of Hans Christian Andersen* (Nyborg 1983; translation mine). This does not imply, however, that the psychological connections that Eigil Nyborg describes are not there. On the contrary:

3. Cf. Chapter 4, pp. 67-71.

they are present and they influence the reader. They are part of what makes Andersen's fairy tales so captivating—even though the author and the majority of his readers may not have become aware of this.

This reference to the fairy tales of Hans Christian Andersen is not meant as a direct parallel to the Baal-cycle. It is, however, a very good example of the fact that a story may contain significant elements without the author being aware of it. We cannot know from a piece of literature alone whether the author was conscious about any given element in the narrative that we might happen to isolate in a literary analysis. What we find in a text is thus not necessarily part of the author's ideology.

Thus from the text of the Ugaritic Baal-cycle we cannot conclude that the anticultic potential that is obviously present in it corresponds to an anticultic ideology, even if this could well have been the case. We simply know too little about the intellectual and/or theological views that were held in ancient Ugarit to be able to say anything decisive in this connection.

Text, Ideology and Conduct

The reason why this interpretation has not been presented earlier in Ugaritic research is due to a sentimental view of humanity in the ancient Near East. According to this view, correspondence between word and action is characteristic of the earliest, naturally unspoiled, human beings. Individual words and scenes in the myth must therefore have had their counterpart in concrete actions, for example, in the cult.[4] Because of this widely accepted view, scholars have been able to construe the Baal-cycle as a cultic text without really presenting any evidence in support of this. Scholars have simply forgotten to distinguish between the inner 'reality' of the text and the outer reality of 'real' life. The inner reality of the Baal-cycle has not necessarily had any connection to or has resulted in any particular conduct in the outer reality (cult or society).

If presented in a rather schematic way, one might say that the adherents of the cultic interpretation think in two closely interrelated levels (A), whereas I suggest we will have to think in three levels (B):

4. Thus, for instance, Pallis, in a paragraph on 'the original form of the *Akītu* festival in the primitive Babylonian agricultural civilization' writes: '...at the stages with which we are dealing, conception and action are merely two aspects of the same matter' (1926: 302). Cf. also my comments on Gaster, pp. 40-52.

(A)
Text   In this case, 'text' refers to the Ugaritic Baal-cycle, that is,
             the clay tablets of the Baal-cycle. The words of this text
             were but one aspect of the text's reality, the performance of
             it being the other.

Conduct   This refers to the enactment of the text. Words correspond
             to actions, actions to words.

(B)
Text   In this case, 'text' refers to the Ugaritic Baal-cycle, that is,
             the clay tablets of the Baal-cycle.

Ideology   The ideology means that the text may be interpreted in dif-
             ferent ways. The various interpretations need not correspond
             to each other. On a more basic level, the Baal-cycle may be
             said to be a story, and it may be that there is no more to it
             than that. It could be claimed that the text is biased, that it
             contains an ideological potential, such as, for example, that
             the text is cultic or anticultic in nature. The author and his
             audience/readers may never have realized this potential. If,
             however, they were aware of this ideological potential we
             might be able to describe the author's ideology to some
             extent.

Conduct   In the case of the Baal-cycle there is a diminutive chance
             that we might have something reasonable to say about the
             ideology of its author. Did anyone ever act according to this
             (presumed) ideology—whether it was cultic or anticultic?
             Actual conduct (of a person, of a group of persons or of
             society as a whole) may or may not be linked to the ideo-
             logy of a particular text.

In very general terms there are three possible ways of reconstructing
the relation between ideology and conduct: conduct corresponds to the
ideology; conduct is opposed to the ideology; or there is no particular
relation between conduct and ideology. The following examples are
meant to illustrate what that entails in our context.

(1) *Correspondence between ideology and conduct.* This would be
the case if the Baal-cycle were a libretto for a drama enacted in the cult
and that every scene and character in the epic corresponded to scenes

and performers in the cult. Correspondence between ideology and conduct would also be the case if the Baal-cycle were an anticultic manifesto and the members of a religious movement were acting according
to this ideology.

(2) *Ideology and conduct are conflicting.* This would be the case if
the Baal-cycle were an anticultic manifesto. The conflicting conduct
would be the cultic activities that the text opposed.

(3) *No relation between ideology and conduct.* The Baal-cycle is not
a cult libretto. The recitation of it in front of a passively listening audience has not evoked any particular social conduct at all.

We need to bear these, in a way very elementary, distinctions in mind
when reconstructing the societies of antiquity (mainly) from texts. We
cannot assume, as do the advocates of cultic interpretations, that correspondence between ideology and conduct was part and parcel of life in
antiquity. True, it is difficult to give examples of a lack of correspondence between 'word and action' in antiquity, since what has been
handed down to us are mainly texts, that is, ideologies. The *aqht-* and
krt-epics may provide us with good examples, if Liverani is right in his
interpretation. The ideal of the king as the righteous judge who sits in
the gate and listens to the cause of the orphans has little to do with the
complicated bureaucracy attested through a wealth of Ugaritic administrative texts (Liverani 1970: 869).

The Sacred and the Profane Spheres

The attentive reader may have noticed that I do occasionally presuppose a distinction between the sacred and the profane spheres—a dif-
ferentiation which was unknown in antiquity, or so it is commonly
claimed.

The idea of the unity of the sacred and profane spheres is so widely
accepted that Niels Peter Lemche presents the idea as a fact in his book
Ancient Israel: A New History of Israelite Society (Lemche 1988: 34
n. 1). Lemche knows, however, that this understanding needs revision.
In a paragraph on the function of the king in Ugaritic religion he says,
discussing the traditional interpretation of sacral kingship,

> ...there is nothing in these documents [i.e. the administrative documents
> from Ugarit] to suggest that the king regarded himself as divine, as is
> obvious from his titulature, which is simply 'NN, king of Ugarit, son of
> NN, king of Ugarit'. Furthermore, the role of the king in the business life

of a trading community like Ugarit is hard to reconcile with notions of the sacral significance of the monarchy which modern historians of religion have advocated.

There are a number of possible explanations for the discrepancies between the epic poems and the administrative texts. One is that the administration and populace of ancient Ugarit were entirely able to distinguish between the king *qua* administrator and the king *qua* cult leader. In other words, that people were able to keep these two spheres, the sacred and the profane, logically separate from one another. However, this conflicts with all that we otherwise happen to know about pre-classical logic (the so-called 'pensée sauvage'), which ordinarily forms a logical system in which the sacred and the profane are combined as a series of interconnected levels which reciprocally influence one another (Lemche 1988: 206).

Hypotheses about the cultic functions of the king have often been exaggerated and based on very little evidence. Gray, for instance, writes on 'sacral kingship' against the background of the function and epithets of the king in texts such as *aqht* and *krt* (Gray 1969).[5] Liverani has presented a more fruitful understanding of the epic poems from Ugarit (Liverani 1970).

It seems evident that the king played some kind of role in the cult. Seen against the background of the ritual texts, however, this role seems to have been quite small. Tarragon concludes:

> In order to make out the concrete practice of the kings of Ugarit as it is revealed in the liturgies one would not have to go far afield: in a certain number of rituals the king acts as the principal agent of the cult. What he does is relatively limited. He proceeds to the rite of purification by means of lustration, he is desacralized at the setting of the sun; one brings before him, in the royal palace, statuettes of certain deities, including those of the dynastic *gtrm*, and he worships them by visiting them and grasping them. One cannot be more precise. Let us add to this the apparently passive presence of the king and queen in a public rite which unifies the entire population of Ugarit, a rite in the course of which singing takes place and a sheep and an ass are sacrificed. It is with such facts as I have summarized here that the theory of 'sacral kingship' should be confronted (1980: 125-26).[6]

5. A critical review of Gray's article may be found in Tarragon 1980: 120-23.
6. 'A prendre la pratique concrète des rois d'Ugarit, telle que les textes liturgiques nous la révèlent, on ne peut aller guère plus loin que ceci : le roi agit dans un certain nombre de rituels comme agent principal du culte. Ce qu'il fait est relativement limité. Il procède au rite de purification par lustration, il est désacralisé au coucher du soleil ; on apporte devant lui, au palais royal, les statuettes de

Tarragon, however, explains the vast difference between the royal ideology of the epic texts and the ritual texts in terms of time: the epic texts belong to an earlier time, hence the discrepancy. 'The distance between the royal ideology of the literary texts of Keret and Danel-Aqhat and that of the rituals and lists of sacrifices reveals the chronological distance which separates them' (Tarragon 1980: 141).[7] On this point Tarragon does not differ much from Gray, who dates *aqht* and *krt* to a 'heroic age', sometime around 2000 BCE (Gray 1969: 293). I believe it is far better to follow Liverani and let *aqht* and *krt* belong to the world of the fairy tale.

Kingship in ancient Syria was administrative in character. Thus the cultic role of the king was but one of his many tasks.[8] The king is a character in the political and social game; his power is limited by powers from above, from the court milieu and from below (cf. Liverani 1974b: 347-56): from above from the high king who could dismiss and judge his vassals; from members of the court—either nobility or the members of the royal family could dethrone the king; and from below, where rebellion was a constant threat. Rebellion could take place in the literal sense of the word, or it could consist in fleeing—which was especially common among peasants (cf. Liverani 1965). The human character of kingship was thus not concealed from the members of society.

In Egypt the concept of kingship was totally different. The notion of Pharaoh's divinity was the basis of a political ideology according to which Pharaoh could not possibly have obligations towards his subjects. Each and every subject owed it to Pharaoh to do his duty without being able to demand anything in recompense. This was true for the civil servants as well as for the vassal kings. This conception of deity clashed with a totally different ideology in the Syro–Palestinian area,

---

certaines divinités, dont celles de *gṯrm* dynastiques, et il les vénère en leur rendant visite et en les saisissant. On ne peut préciser plus. Ajoutons à cela la présence, plus passive apparemment, du roi et de la reine dans un rite public réunissant toute la population d'Ugarit, rite au cours duquel on chante et on offre un mouton et un âne. C'est avec ces données, ici résumées, que doit être confrontée la théorie du "sacral kingship"'.

7. 'L'écart entre l'idéologie royale des textes littéraires de Keret et Danel-Aqhat et celle des rituels et listes d'offrandes révèle la distance chronologique qui les sépare'.

8. Cf. Heltzer's conclusion in Heltzer 1982: 179-80.

where we find an ideology that was based on a contractual relationship between ruler and subject. The subject was, of course, obliged to yield certain contributions either in terms of money, goods or labour, but in return he could expect a degree of protection from his master. Liverani has dealt intensively with the clash between these two political conceptions (Liverani 1967b); among the Amarna letters, Rib-Adda's correspondence is a very good example of the contrast between the two ideologies (cf. Liverani 1971, 1974a).

This Egyptian ideology had its background in the idea of Pharaoh as divine. The reason that this political concept clashed with the ideology dominant in the Syro–Palestinian area is probably that the position of the king was different. The king in the Syro–Palestinian area was regarded as a human being, as can be seen from his title (as mentioned above), and from the fact that he is a person with whom it is possible to establish contractual relations: in recompense for a certain contribution one can expect a certain reciprocal contribution.[9]

Thus we need to revise the idea that the sacred and the profane spheres comprised a single whole in ancient oriental societies. This is reflected in the conception of the king—as Liverani has demonstrated—and in the literary production in Ugarit: the existence of such great literary works as the *aqht*- and *krt*-epics, that is, texts which did not have their *Sitz im Leben* in the cult; and perhaps also the Baal-cycle, a text that one cannot with any certainty regard as a cult-text; these may be seen as literary results of a culture detached from the religious sphere. Seen in this light, the anti-cultic potential of the Baal-cycle is much less astounding. The fact that the author of the Baal-cycle—one of the earliest examples of literature we possess—has borrowed imagery from the religious sphere (gods, etc.) is not surprising. His point of departure was, naturally enough, the tradition he was rooted in.

The contrary development (that fictional literature in a very general meaning of the word becomes religious literature in a more narrow sense of the word) may also occur. This is, for instance, the case with the biblical flood story (Gen. 6.5–8.22), which is quite obviously dependent on Mesopotamian flood stories. This tradition was part of

9.   The difference between Egyptian and Mesopotamian royal ideology is described by Frankfort (Frankfort 1978, cf. esp. Kramer's preface: v-viii, and the Introduction, esp. 5-6), by Gadd (Gadd 1948: 33-34) and, of course, by Liverani.

literary creations such as, for instance, the epic of Gilgamesh before it
became part of the biblical narrative.[10]

Ideology and Psychology

There is a tendency in more recent Old Testament scholarship to
question the historicity of the majority of the narratives in the Old Testament. More and more, the Old Testament is being construed as ideological writing which is to give identity to a group of exiled
'Canaanites', or Jews,[11] and to justify their territorial demands in
Palestine.

Already in 1980 Liverani wrote that a possible explanatory model
concerning the origins of Israel could be constructed by pushing the
date of the Israelite ethnogenesis forward to exilic or postexilic times,
since the settlement traditions of the Old Testament would have to be
regarded as part of an origin construction of a later period (Liverani
1980: 30-31).[12] The early history of Israel (i.e. the history before
c. 1000 BCE) has intensively been studied by Niels Peter Lemche
(Lemche 1972, 1985, 1986). One of the results of his investigations is
that the Old Testament, by and large, cannot be used as a source for a
reconstruction of the early history of Israel. Such a reconstruction
would have to be based on written and archaeological sources outside
of the Old Testament. Such a multidisciplinary investigation has been
undertaken by Thomas L. Thompson. Concerning the formation of the
Old Testament, Thompson's conclusion runs (repeated here in a rather
simplified form) that the Old Testament came into being in the Persian
era as a kind of identity-creating survival literature. Thompson admits,
however, that 'the tradition truly comes from the past: fragments of
memory: written and oral, chains of narrative, complex literary works,
administrative records', etc. (Thompson 1992: 421). The governing
principle for the literary combination of these traditions is, however,
the Babylonian exile: 'Radical trauma of exile is used as a *literary
paradigm* in terms of which both newly formed tradition and its

10. An outline of the flood traditions can be found in Westermann's excursus in
Westermann 1974: 537-45.

11. That the Israelites were originally Canaanites is one of the results of the
new reconstructions of the history of Israel, cf. Lemche 1985, 1991.

12. Ethnogenesis (*terminus technicus* for the origin of a people) is Liverani's
own expression.

collectors acquired identity as Israel' (Thompson 1992: 422; emphasis mine). Philip R. Davies, in his book *In Search of 'Ancient Israel'*, followed Thompson in this view and gave some refreshing considerations on the coming into being of biblical literature (Davies 1992; cf. also Lemche 1992).

More specific examples of the re-evaluation of the historicity of the Old Testament narratives may be mentioned. Thus Van Seters believes that the succession narrative (2 Sam. 9–20; 1 Kgs 1–2) is 'a post-Dtr addition to the history of David from the postexilic period' (Van Seters 1983: 290). Frederick Harris Cryer has made even more precise statements about it:

> For nearly one generation the succession narrative has been seen as an exemplary model of the history writing which—so it has been surmised—came into being during the Israelite monarchy in order to sustain, make propaganda for and justify the Davidic royal house. A number of features in this story, however, make it necessary that we construe it as an attempt of a much later time to compose a Jewish answer to the career of Alexander the Great and to the literature which flourished in the wake of the conquests of Alexander.[13]

Archaeological investigations may support such views: Jamieson-Drake concludes in his *Scribes and Schools in Monarchic Judah*, that the Judaean state could not have come into existence before the eighth century BCE, and that it ceased to exist in the sixth century BCE. The Davidic empire seems never to have existed:

> There is little evidence that Judah began to function as a state at all prior to the tremendous increases in population, building, production, centralization and specialization which began to appear in the 8th century...The primary problem is one of scale: the levels of production and population were just too small in 10th-century Judah to suggest the presence of the full-scale state; they seem more appropriate to a chiefdom, generally...However, even if we were to ignore this fact and evaluate the society in this region on the basis of complexity alone, the amount of evidence for material centralization or full-time craft specialization is small indeed. Under our polythetic classification scheme, Judah was a small state in the 8th–7th centuries, but not before (1991: 138-39).[14]

13. Quoted from the lecture list of the Theological Faculty, the University of Copenhagen, spring 1992 (my translation). This is also the subject of Cryer's forthcoming monograph.

14. One of the main problems in Jamieson-Drake's book is, of course, the nature of his source material, or perhaps rather the lack of solid material for his

The view of history quoted above,[15] and especially the concept of the Old Testament as an ideological work, must influence our understanding of the psychology of the ancient semites. One of the classic works in this area is Johannes Pedersen's *Israel I–II* and *Israel III–IV* (Pedersen 1920, 1934 [English editions 1926, 1940]). Pedersen's view on Israelite psychology is to a very high degree based on an interpretation of the Old Testament texts. Thoughts, various turns of speech, and structures in family and society in the Old Testament are perceived by Pedersen as genuine expressions of the way of thinking of 'the ancients'. Much credit is to be given to Pedersen, of course. Pedersen is thus probably right in maintaining that strong family ties were present in semitic societies in antiquity. But is he also right in saying that these intense feelings of community were extended and encompassed the whole people? The 'deuteronomists' would probably have appreciated the following quote from Pedersen, but one wonders whether the ordinary 'Israelite' man or woman would have felt that this is a true description of their way of thinking and speaking:

> *'am* thus means the same as the father's house and the family, because it arises out of kinship. The three definitions centre on the same idea: the father, the rise of the family. The father's house is most closely attached to him, the 'family' extends further, and the 'people of kinsmen' furthest of all; it is the most flexible of the three conceptions, seeing that it denotes the entirety extending the furthest: the nation, the people. It denotes all of those who take part in the whole of the common history. This totality acquired firmness and strength during the period of the fusion and the fights with the foreign people in and outside Canaan, and during the time of the monarchy it was further established. It became the unit of greatest importance besides the family (Pedersen 1926: 56-57).

I wonder if the members of 'ordinary' families in ancient Israel would agree with this characterization.

If the Old Testament—roughly speaking—came into being in an attempt at creating an Israelite consciousness and feeling of community, we cannot use the ideology contained in it to describe the way of thinking of the ancient semites in general. What we perhaps *can* say is how the authors of the Old Testament wished them to think.

---

conclusions. Anyway, it is clear that the lack of evidence is certainly not in favour of the existence of a Davidic empire.

15. This view of history is not, of course, the only one existing in modern Old Testament scholarship. A contrasting view can be found in, e.g., de Moor 1990.

An investigation of the psychology of the ancient semites in the period Pedersen deals with would need a much larger and more diverse textual material from the Syro–Palestinian area in the second first half of the first millennium than we actually possess (cf. the sparse material in, e.g., *KAI*).

The Dating of the Old Testament Psalms: An Insoluble Problem

An assessment of Mowinckel's theory about the enthronement festival of Yahweh must be determined to a very high degree by the dating of the Old Testament psalms, which is an almost impossible task. Since the psalms contain hardly any historical information at all, dating them would be determined by one's view on the history of Israel and its history of religion.

The view of Israel's history presented above may influence the dating of the Old Testament psalms, although there has not as yet been any attempt made to describe the consequences of the new historical research for the psalms. A likely consequence of this tendency in historical research is a late dating of most of the psalms.[16]

Dating the psalms of the Old Testament is, of course, a historical problem. In the following, I shall present a brief example of the consequences the lack of a secure date may have for the interpretation of the psalms.

The example in question is the frequent use of the notion of *enemies* in the psalms.[17] It is impossible to reconstruct with any degree of

---

16. As can be seen in, e.g., Fohrer 1979: 307-18.

17. The *enemies* is a much debated issue in psalm research. Mowinckel, in his early works, distinguished between national psalms of lamentation and individual psalms of lamentation. In the first mentioned group of psalms the enemies are national enemies, i.e. neighbouring peoples occasionally mentioned by name as in Ps. 83 (cf. Mowinckel 1921: 77). In the individual psalms of lamentation, however, the *enemies* is synonymous with the evildoers, the פֹּעֲלֵי אָוֶן, who were regarded as the cause of the misery of the lamenting person (Mowinckel 1921: 77-78, 81). Mowinckel has later reviewed these theories after being influenced by Harris Birkeland: '…H. Birkeland, *Die Feinde des Individums* [*Individuums*] *in der israelitischen Psalmenliteratur…*has given the necessary corrections of my very one-sided view in *Psalmenstudien I*' (Mowinckel 1951b: 205).

'Das Irrtum war… dass ich an Gunkels rein mechanischer Unterscheidung zwischen Ich-Psalmen und Wir-Psalmen noch festhielt, und infolgedessen sämtliche Ich-Klagepsalmen als Krankheitspsalmen deutete. Durch H. Birkelands *Die*

certainty the possible concrete reality behind this notion, just as it is impossible to reconstruct the reality behind the psalms altogether. One might be tempted to interpret the 'enemies' as the enemies of the individual supplicant, or perhaps the 'enemies of the faith'. Fohrer is a representative of this interpretation. Fohrer believes that the question of 'enemies' has to do with the fact of 'personal opposition, which in daily life is not a rare phenomenon, which makes sense of the identification of the victim of hostility with the pious and his/her opponent with the impious' (1979: 289).[18]

Fohrer's interpretation is justified even if concrete historical enemies should happen to lie behind the notion of 'enemies' in the psalms. The possible historical event was forgotten and it is the more universal character of the psalms that has made them worthy of preservation. One might seek in one's interpretation to stress this universal aspect of the psalms. One might equally well surmise that certain psalms once had a historical or cultic *Sitz im Leben*, but we completely lack the necessary data to determine this *Sitz im Leben* with any precision. The history of research shows that any attempt at finding the *Sitz im Leben* of the Old Testament psalms is based on more or less hypothetical constructions.

The difficulty of understanding an expression like the *enemies* in the psalms is not unlike the one which occurs whenever we attempt to interpret a prophetic saying. Kirsten Nielsen writes on this subject:

> We must…underline the original character of topical preaching of these words (without dismissing the universal truths such topical preaching might contain), and then at the same time call attention to the tendency towards universalization and dogmatization inherent in the actual communicating of the prophetic preaching beyond the concrete situation in which the preaching arose (1976: 229; my translation).

Feinde des Individuums in der israelitischen Psalmenliteratur, Oslo 1933, habe ich mich darüber belehren lassen, dass es viele Ich-Klagepsalmen, darunter besonders die sogenannten Vertrauens-Psalmen, in denen die Not nur noch als drohende Gefahr vor den Augen des Betenden steht, gibt, in denen das Ich nicht ein beliebiger "Jedermann", sondern der König des Volkes ist, und die Feinde somit nationaler, politischer Art sind, die aber in Ausdrücken, die ursprünglich Zauberer und Dämonen bezeichnen, charakterisiert werden…' (Mowinckel 1961, unpaginated Preface).

18. 'persönliche Gegnerschaft, wie sie im täglichen Leben nicht eben selten ist, wozu durchweg die Gleichsetzung der Angefeindeten mit den Frommen und der Gegner mit den Unfrommen tritt'.

This problem, which is a general problem in exegesis (cf. Nielsen 1976: 229-30) also occurs in connection with the interpretation of the notion of the *enemies*.

Fohrer's interpretation of the expression *enemies* is thus not wrong; it is just not the whole 'truth' about the text. This characterization fits any literary interpretation of Biblical texts. It is not meant as a negative evaluation of literary approaches to biblical texts—on the contrary, it is meant as a more explicit formulation of the limits of these methods.

Acceptance or dismissal of Mowinckel's theories depends on one's views of theological or humanistic research and the demands one makes on a hypothesis. Mowinckel's attitude is clearly expressed in *Psalmenstudien II*:

> A hypothesis is 'true' if it is able satisfactorily and without remainder to explain the facts of a matter. Our hypothesis, that the enthronement psalms are cultic psalms and that a corresponding feast must once have existed, is then to be regarded as proven if we succeed in explaining satisfactorily the peculiarities of the psalms in question (1922: 44).[19]

B. Duhm is a good representative of the opposite attitude: 'Certainty and necessity are achieved when, in the course of striving, one is forced to abandon a great deal. We ought rather to know somewhat less in order to enjoy greater certainty about what one knows. It therefore seems better to me not to offer any historical explanation than an uncertain one' (quotation from Bernhardt 1961: 22).[20] The author of this book shares this attitude.

19. 'Eine Hypotese ist "wahr", wenn sie die vorliegende Tatsachen befriedigend und restlos zu erklären vermag. Unsere Hypotese, daß die Thronbesteigungspsalmen Kultpsalmen sind und daß es somit einmal ein dementsprechendes Fest gegeben haben muß, muß dann als bewiesen gelten, wenn es uns gelingt, aus ihr die Eigentümlichkeiten der erwähnten Psalmen befriedigend zu erklären.'
20. 'Sicherheit und Nothwendigkeit ist das, wonach man bei jeder Forschung, und also auch bei der Erklärung zuerst streben und dem man manchens Andere aufopfern muß. Lieber wisse man etwas weniger, das aber, was man weiß, mit größerer Gewißheit! Daher scheint es mir besser, keine historische Erklärung zu geben, als eine unsichere.'

BIBLIOGRAPHY

Aartun, Kjell
1974   *Die Partikeln des Ugaritischen* (AOAT, 21.1; Kevelaer: Verlag Butzon &
            Bercker; Neukirchen–Vluyn: Neukirchener Verlag).
Abou-Assaf, Ali, Pierre Bordreuil and Alan R. Millard
1982   *La Statue de Tell Fekherye et son inscription bilingue assyro-araméenne*
            (Etudes Assyriologiques, 7; Paris: Editions Recherche sur les civilisa-
            tions).
Albright, William Foxwell
1961   'The Role of the Canaanites in the History of Civilization', in Wright
            1961: 328-62.
1968   *Yahweh and the Gods of Canaan: A Historical Analysis of Two Contrast-
            ing Faiths* (The Jordan Lectures in Comparative Religion 1965; London:
            Athlone Press; repr. Winona Lake, IN: Eisenbrauns; 1978, 1990).
Baudissin, Wolf Wilhelm Graf
1911   *Adonis und Esmun: Eine Untersuchung zur Geschichte des Glaubens an
            Auferstehungsgötter und an Heilgötter* (Leipzig: J.C. Hinrichs).
Bernhardt, Karl-Heinz
1961   *Das Problem der altorientalischen Königsideologie im Alten Testament:
            Unter besondere Berücksichtigung der Geschichte der Psalmenexegese
            dargestellt und kritisch gewürdigt* (VTSup,8; Leiden: E.J. Brill).
1967   'Aschera in Ugarit und im Alten Testament', *MIO*, 13: 163-74.
Birkeland, Harris
1933   *Die Feinde des Individuums in der israelitischen Psalmenliteratur: Ein
            Beitrag zur Kenntnis der semitischen Literatur- und religionsgeschichte*
            (Oslo: Grøndahl & Søns Forlag).
Bjerg, Svend
1989   *Karen Blixens teologi* (Aarhus: Anis).
Caquot, André
1969   'Problèmes d'histoire religieuse', in Liverani 1969: 61-76.
Caquot, André and Maurice Sznycer
1980   *Ugaritic Religion* (Iconography of Religions, 15.8; Leiden: E.J. Brill).
Chwolsohn, D.
1856   *Die Ssabier und der Ssabismus* (2 vols.; St Petersburg: Buchdruckerei der
            kaiserlichen Akademie der Wissenschaften).
Cunchillos Ylarri, Jesús-Luis
1984   'Expresiones de la fe y la piedad cotidianas en las salutaciones de las car-
            tas de Ugarit', in N. Fernandez Marcos *et al.* (eds.), *Simposio Bíblico
            Español, Salamanca 1982* (Madrid: Universidad Complutense): 115-28.

1985   'La foi et la piété quotidiennes dans le corps des lettres trouvées à Ugarit', in A. Caquot, S. Légasse and M. Tardieu (eds.), *Mélanges bibliques et orientaux en l'honneur de M. Mathias Delcor* (AOAT, 215; Kevelaer: Verlag Butzon & Bercker; Neukirchen–Vluyn: Neukirchener Verlag): 69-77.

Dahl, Nils A.
1988   'Sigmund Mowinckel: Historian of Religion and Theologian', in *SJOT* 2: 8-22.

Dalman, Gustaf
1928   *Arbeit und Sitte in Palästina* (7 vols.; BFCT, 2; Gütersloh: C. Bertelsmann).

Davies, Philip R.
1992   *In Search of 'Ancient Israel'* (JSOTSup, 148; Sheffield: Sheffield Academic Press).

Fohrer, Georg
1979   *Einleitung in das Alte Testament: Begründet von Ernst Sellin, neubearbeitet von Georg Fohrer* (Heidelberg: Quelle & Meyer, 12th edn).

Frankfort, Henri
1951   *The Problem of Similarity in Ancient Near Eastern Religions: The Frazer Lecture 1950* (Oxford: Clarendon Press).
1978   *Kingship and the Gods: A Study of Ancient Near Eastern Religion as the Integration of Society and Nature. With a New Preface by Samuel Noah Kramer* (Chicago: University of Chicago Press, 2nd edn [1st edn 1948]).

Frazer, James George
1911   *The Golden Bough: A Study in Magic and Religion* (13 vols.; London: Macmillan, 3rd edn).

Frymer-Kensky, Tikva
1983   'The Tribulations of Marduk: The So-Called "Marduk Ordeal Text"', *JAOS* 103: 131-41.

Gadd, Cyril John
1948   *Ideas of Divine Rule in the Ancient East: The Schweich Lectures of the British Academy 1945* (London: Oxford University Press).

Garelli, Paul (ed.)
1974   *Le palais et la royauté (Archéologie et Civilisation): XIXe Rencontre Assyriologique Internationale* (Paris: Paul Geuthner).

Gaster, Theodor Herzl
1950   *Thespis: Ritual, Myth and Drama in the Ancient Near East* (New York: Henry Schuman).
1961   *Thespis: Ritual, Myth and Drama in the Ancient Near East* (New York: Doubleday, 2nd rev. edn).

George, A.R.
1993   *House Most High: The Temples of Ancient Mesopotamia* (Mesopotamian Civilizations, 5; Winona Lake, IN: Eisenbrauns).

Gese, Hartmut
1970   'Die Religionen Altsyriens', in Gese, Höfner and Rudolph 1970: 1-232.

Gese, Hartmut, Maria Höfner and Kurt Rudolph
1970   *Die Religionen Altsyriens, Altarabiens und der Mandäer* (Die Religionen
           der Menschheit, 10.2; ed. Christel Matthias Schröder; Stuttgart: Kohl-
           hammer).
Gibson, J.C.L.
1978   *Canaanite Myths and Legends: Originally Edited by G.R. Driver*
           (Edinburgh: T. & T. Clark).
Gray, John
1969   'Sacral Kingship in Ugarit', in *Ug*: 289-302.
Greenfield, Jonas C.
1984   'A Touch of Eden', in *Festschrift J. Duchesne-Guillemin* (Acta Iranica,
           23; Hommages et opera minora, 9; Leiden: E.J. Brill): 219-24.
Gunkel, Hermann
1913a   *Reden und Aufsätze* (Göttingen: Vandenhoeck & Ruprecht).
1913b   'Die Endhoffnung der Psalmisten', in Gunkel 1913a: 123-30.
1933   *Einleitung in die Psalmen: Die Gattungen der religiösen Lyrik Israels. Zu
           Ende geführt von Joachim Begrich* (HKAT, 2; Göttingen: Vandenhoeck
           & Ruprecht).
Heltzer, Michael
1982   *The Internal Organization of the Kingdom of Ugarit: Royal Service-
           system, Taxes, Royal Economy, Army and Administration* (Wiesbaden:
           Reichert).
Hooke, S.H.
1962   *Babylonian and Assyrian Religion* (London: Hutchinson).
Hooke, S.H. (ed.)
1933   *Myth and Ritual: Essays on the Myth and Ritual of the Hebrews in Rela-
           tion to the Culture Pattern of the Ancient East* (London: Oxford Univer-
           sity Press).
1935   *The Labyrinth: Further Studies in the Relation between Myth and Ritual*
           (London: SPCK).
1958   *Myth, Ritual, and Kingship: Essays on the Theory and Practice of King-
           ship in the Ancient Near East and in Israel* (Oxford: Clarendon Press).
Hvidberg, Flemming Friis
1938   *Graad og Latter i Det gamle Testamente: En Studie i kanaanæisk-
           israelitisk Religion. Festskrift udgivet af Københavns Universitet i
           anledning af Universitetets Aarsfest November 1938* (Copenhagen:
           G.E.C. Gad).
1962   *Weeping and Laughter in the Old Testament: A Study of Canaanite–
           Israelite Religion* (ed. and rev. F. Løkkegaard; trans. Niels Haislund;
           Leiden: E.J. Brill; Copenhagen: Nyt Nordisk Forlag, Arnold Busck).
Hvidberg-Hansen, Finn O.
1990   *Kana'anæiske myter og legender: Tekster fra Ras Shamra-Ugarit. Dansk
           oversættelse med kommentar* (2 vols.; Aarhus: Aarhus Universitets-
           forlag).
Jacobsen, Thorkild
1970   'Toward the Image of Tammuz', in Jacobsen and Moran 1970: 73-103.

Jacobsen, Thorkild and William L. Moran (eds.)
1970   *Toward the Image of Tammuz and Other Essays on Mesopotamian History and Culture: Edited by William L. Moran* (Harvard Semitic Series, 21; Cambridge, MA: Harvard University Press).

Jamieson-Drake, David W.
1991   *Scribes and Schools in Monarchic Judah: A Socio-Archeological Approach* (JSOTSup, 109; SWBA, 9; Sheffield: Almond Press).

Jeppesen, Knud
1988   'The Day of Yahweh in Mowinckel's Conception Reviewed', *SJOT* 2: 42-55.

Kapelrud, Arvid S.
1940   'Jahves tronstigningsfest og funnene i Ras Sjamra', *NorTT* 41: 38-58.
1952   *Baal in the Ras Shamra Texts* (Copenhagen: G.E.C. Gad).
1963   *The Ras Shamra Discoveries and the Old Testament* (Norman, OK: University of Oklahoma Press).
1969   *The Violent Goddess: Anat in the Ras Shamra Texts* (Oslo: Universitetsforlaget).
1973   *Vår Konge er Baal: Fruktbarhetsguden Baal i Ras Sjamra-tekstene* (Oslo: Universitetsforlaget).

Kinet, Dirk
1978   'Theologische Reflexion im ugaritischen Baal-Zyklus', *BZ* 22: 236-44.

Labat, René
1976   *Manuel d'épigraphie akkadienne (Signes, Syllabaire, Idéogrammes): Nouvelle édition, revue et corrigée par Florence Malbran-Labat* (Paris: Geuthner, 5th edn).

Langdon, Stephan
1923   *The Babylonian Epic of Creation* (Oxford: Clarendon Press).
1924   *Excavations at Kish, I* (4 vols.; Paris: Paul Geuthner).
1928   'Relics of Sumer's First Capital after the Flood: Discoveries at Kish. Chariots and Oxen of 3500 BC; and a Woman's Splendid Jewels', *The Illustrated London News* June 2: 991.

Langhe, Robert de
1958   'Myth, Ritual, and Kingship in The Ras Shamra Tablets', in Hooke 1958. 122-48.

Lemche, Niels Peter
1972   *Israel i dommertiden: En oversigt over diskussionen om Martin Noths 'Das System der zwölf Stämme Israels'* (Tekst & Tolkning, 4; Copenhagen: G.E.C. Gad).
1985   *Early Israel: Anthropological and Historical Studies on the Israelite Society Before the Monarchy* (VTSup, 37; Leiden: E.J. Brill).
1986   *Det gamle Israel: Det israelitiske samfund fra sammenbruddet af bronzealderkulturen til hellenistisk tid* (Aarhus: Anis; 2nd edn).
1988   *Ancient Israel: A New History of Israelite Society* (The Biblical Seminar, 5; Sheffield: JSOT Press).
1991   *The Canaanites and their Land: The Tradition of the Canaanites* (JSOTSup, 110; Sheffield: JSOT Press).
1993   'The Old Testament –A Hellenistic Book', *SJOT* 7: 163-93.

Lipiński, Éduard
1962   *Les Psaumes de la Royauté de Yahvé dans l'exégèse moderne* (Sylloge
            Excerptorum e dissertationibus ad gradum doctoris in Sacra Theologia
            vel in Iure canonico consequendum conscriptis, 38.3; Louvain: Publica-
            tions Universitaires de Louvain).
Liverani, Mario
1965   'Il fuoruscitismo in Siria nella tarda età del bronzo', *Rivista Storica Ital-
            iana* 77: 315-36.
1967a   '"Ma nel settimo anno..."', in Giorgio Buccellati (ed.), *Studi sull'Ori-
            ente e la Bibbia offerti al P. Giovanni Rinaldi nel 60° compleanno*
            (Genova): 49-53.
1967b   'Contrasti e confluenze di concezioni politiche nell'età di El-Amarna', *RA*
            61: 1-18.
1970   'L'epica ugaritica nel suo contesto storico e letterario', in *Atti del con-
            vegno internazionale sul tema: La poesia epica e la sua formazione*
            (Problemi attuali di scienza e di cultura, 139; Rome: Accademia
            Nazionale dei Lincei): 859-69.
1971   'Le lettere del Faraone a Rib-Adda', *OrAnt* 10: 253-68.
1974a   'Rib-Adda, giusto sofferente', *Altorientalische Forschungen* 1; *Schriften
            zur Geschichte und Kultur des Alten Orients* 11: 175-205.
1974b   'La royauté syrienne de l'âge du bronze récent', in Garelli 1974: 329-56.
1980   'Le "Origini" d'Israele progetto irrealizzabile di recerca etnogenetica',
            RivB 28: 9-31.
1988   'Il primo piano degli archivi di Ugarit', in P. Xella (ed.), *Cananea
            Selecta: Festschrift für Oswald Loretz zum 60. Geburtstag* (Studi epi-
            grafici e linguistici sul Vicino Oriente antico, 5; Verona: Essedue Edi-
            zioni): 121-42.
1993   *Mario Liverani: Artikler i oversættelse ved Niels Peter Lemche* (2 vols.;
            trans. Niels Peter Lemche; Copenhagen: private edn, 2nd edn).
Liverani, Mario (ed.)
1969   *La Siria nel Tardo Bronzo* (Orientis antiqvi collectio, 9; Rome: Centro
            per le Antichità e la Storia dell'arte del Vicino Oriente).
Livingstone, Alasdair
1986   *Mystical and Mythological Explanatory Works of Assyrian and Babylo-
            nian Scholars* (Oxford: Clarendon Press).
1989   *Court Poetry and Literary Miscellanea* (State Archives of Assyria, 3;
            Helsinki: Helsinki University Press).
Margalit, Baruch
1980   *A Matter of 'Life' and 'Death': A Study of the Baal-Mot Epic (CTA 4-5-
            6)* (AOAT, 206; Kevelaer: Verlag Butzon & Bercker; Neukirchen–Vluyn:
            Neukirchener Verlag).
Michelet, S., Sigmund Mowinckel and N. Messel
1929–63   *Det Gamle Testamente* (5 vols.; Oslo: M. Aschehoug & Co.).
Moor, Johannes C. de
1971   *The Seasonal Pattern in the Ugaritic Myth of Ba'lu* (AOAT, 16; Keve-
            laer: Verlag Butzon & Bercker; Neukirchen–Vluyn: Neukirchener Ver-
            lag).

1990   *The Rise of Yahwism: The Roots of Israelite Monotheism* (BETL, 91;
             Leuven: Leuven University Press).

Mowinckel, Sigmund
1921   *Psalmenstudien I: Åwän und die individuellen Klagepsalmen* (Skrifter
             utg. av Vitenskapsselskapet i Kristiania, 4; Kristiania (now Oslo): Jacob
             Dybwad; reprinted in Mowinckel 1961).
1922   *Psalmenstudien II: Das Thronbesteigungsfest Jahwäs und der Ursprung
             der Eschatologie* (Skrifter utg. av Vitenskapsselskapet i Kristiania, 6;
             Kristiania (now Oslo): Jacob Dybwad; reprinted in Mowinckel 1961).
1924a   'Det kultiske synspunkt som forskningsprincipp i den gammeltesta-
             mentlige videnskap', *NorTT* 25: 1-23.
1950   *Religion og kultus* (Oslo: Land & Kirke).
1951a   *Offersang og sangoffer: Salmediktningen i Bibelen* (Oslo: H. Aschehoug
             & Co.).
1951b   'Traditionalism and Personality in the Psalms', *HUCA* 23: 205-31
             (reprinted in Mowinckel 1962, Ch. 17).
1953a   *Der achtundsechzigste Psalm* (ANVAO, 2; Oslo: Jacob Dybwad).
1953b   *Religion und Kultus* (Göttingen: Vandenhoeck & Ruprecht).
1955a   *Skriftene: 1. del. Oversatt av Sigmund Mowinckel* (= Michelet, Mow-
             inckel and Messel 1929, IV; Oslo: M. Aschehoug & Co.).
1955b   '"Psalm criticism between 1900 and 1935" (Ugarit and Psalm exegesis)',
             VT 5: 13-33.
1961   *Psalmenstudien I–VI* (Reprinted with a new 'Vorwort' [Preface] and
             'Berichtungen [*read* Berichtigungen] und Ergänzungen' [corrections and
             additions]; Amsterdam: Verlag P. Schippers N.V.; 2nd edn, Amsterdam:
             Verlag P. Schippers N.V., 1966]).
1962   *The Psalms in Israel's Worship* (trans. D.R. Ap-Thomas; 2 vols.; Oxford:
             Basil Blackwell; rev. edn of Mowinckel 1951a).

Nielsen, Kirsten
1976   'Profeternes opgør med kulten', *DTT* 39: 217-30.

Noth, Martin
1958   *Das zweite Buch Mose: Exodus* (ATD, 5; Göttingen: Vandenhoeck &
             Ruprecht).

Nyborg, Eigil
1983   *Den indre linie i H.C. Andersens eventyr: En psykologisk studie*
             (Copenhagen: Gyldendal, 2nd edn).

Oldenburg, Ulf
1969   *The Conflict between El and Ba'al in Canaanite Religion* (Supplement to
             Numen, 3; Leiden: E.J. Brill).

Pallis, Svend Aage
1926   *The Babylonian Akîtu Festival* (Historisk-filologiske Meddelelser udgivne
             af Det Kgl. Danske Videnskabernes Selskab, 12.1; Copenhagen: Høst).

Pedersen, Johannes
1920   *Israel I–II: Sjæleliv og Samfundsliv* (Copenhagen: Poul Branner).
1926   *Israel I–II: Its Life and Culture* (London: Humphrey Milford; Copen-
             hagen: Branner & Korch).
1934   *Israel III–IV: Hellighed og Guddommelighed* (Copenhagen: Poul
             Branner).

1940   *Israel III–IV: Its Life and Culture* (London: Humphrey Milford; Copenhagen: Branner & Korch).

Pedersén, Olof

1985   *Archives and Libraries in the City of Assur: A Survey of the Material from the German Excavations, I* (Uppsala: Almqvist & Wiksell).

1986   *Archives and Libraries in the City of Assur: A Survey of the Material from the German Excavations, II* (Uppsala: Almqvist & Wiksell).

Pongratz-Leisten, Beate

1994   *Ina Šulmi Īrub: Die kulttopographische und ideologische Programmatik der akītu-Prozession in Babylonien und Assyrien in 1. Jahrtausend v. Chr.* (Baghdader Forschungen, 16; Mainz: Verlag Philipp von Zabern).

Reich, Ebbe Kløvedal

1986   *Frederik: En folkebog om N.F.S. Grundtvigs tid og liv* (Copenhagen: Gyldendal, 3rd edn).

Rendtorff, Knud G.

1959   'Sejrshymnen i Exodus 15 og dens forhold til tronbestigelsessalmerne', *DTT* 22: 65-81, 156-71.

Renfroe, F.

1986   'Methodological Considerations Regarding the Use of Arabic in Ugaritic Philology', *UF* 18: 33-74.

Schaeffer, Claude F.-A.

1939   *The Cuneiform Texts of Ras Shamra-Ugarit* (The Schweich Lectures of the British Academy, 1936; London: Oxford University Press).

Schmidt, Hans

1927   *Die Thronfahrt Jahves am Fest der Jahreswende im Alten Israel* (Sammlung gemeinverständlicher Vorträge und Schriften aus dem Gebiet der Theologie und Religionsgeschichte, 122; Tübingen: J.C.B. Mohr).

Smith, Mark S.

1986   'Interpreting the Baal Cycle', *UF* 18: 313-39.

Smith, Sidney

1928   'Assyriological Notes: A Babylonian Fertility Cult', *JRAS* 60: 849-75.

Soden, Wolfram von

1955   'Gibt es ein Zeugnis dafür, daß die Babylonier an die Wiederauferstehung Marduks geglaubt haben?', *ZA* 51: 130-66.

Tarragon, Jean-Michel de

1980   *Le culte à Ugarit d'après les textes de la pratique en cunéiformes alphabétique* (Cahiers de la revue biblique, 19; Paris: J. Gabalda).

Thompson, Thomas L.

1992   *Early History of the Israelite People: From the Written and Archaeological Sources* (Studies in the History of the Ancient Near East, 4; Leiden: E.J. Brill).

Thureau-Dangin, François

1921   *Rituels accadiens* (Paris: Ernest Leroux).

Van Seters, John

1983   *In Search of History: Historiography in the Ancient World and the Origins of Biblical History* (New Haven: Yale University Press).

Wanke, Gunther
1970   '"Eschatologie": Ein Beispiel theologischer Sprachverwirrung', in
            Kerygma und Dogma (Zeitschrift für theologische Forschung und kirch-
            liche Lehre, 16; Göttingen: Vandenhoeck & Ruprecht): 300-12.
Westermann, Claus
1974   *Genesis, I: Genesis 1–11* (BKAT, 1.1; Neukirchen–Vluyn: Neukirchener
            Verlag).
Wright, G.E. (ed.)
1961   *The Bible and the Ancient Near East: Essays in Honor of W.F. Albright*
            (New York: Doubleday).
Zimmern, Heinrich
1918   *Zum babylonischen Neujahrsfest, II* (BSGW, 70.5; Leipzig: B.G.
            Teubner).

INDEXES

INDEX OF REFERENCES

OLD TESTAMENT

JOURNAL FOR THE STUDY OF THE OLD TESTAMENT
SUPPLEMENT SERIES